P9-EGC-898

Gary Lyons

Desert Plants

A CURATOR'S INTRODUCTION

Huntington Library

Cereus huntingtonianus hybrid

to the

HUNTINGTON

DESERT

GARDEN

Aloe 'Henry Huntington'

San Marino, California

Principal photography Gary Lyons, Don Normark, and
  John Sullivan
Additional photography Lisa Blackburn, Ralph Cornell,
  Judith Danner, Bruce Gelvin, Dorothy Gelvin,
  William Hertrich, Bill Thornton, Michael Vassar
Index Jean Patterson
Design Lilli Colton
Printing Typecraft Wood & Jones, Pasadena, CA
First edition

Front cover Agave parryi var. *truncata*
Back cover *Lithops*, golden barrel cactus, *Kalanchoe
  grandiflora*, *Aloe dorotheae*
End sheets The Huntington Desert Garden
Page 1 *Bromelia balansae* 'Heart of Fire'

Huntington Library Press
1151 Oxford Road
San Marino, CA 91108
www.huntington.org

Peggy Park Bernal, *Director*
Susan Green, *Editor*
Jean Patterson, *Promotion and Production Coordinator*

This book is one of a series of publications on the
Huntington Botanical Gardens made possible by a
generous contribution from Helen and Peter Bing.

ISBN (paper) 978-0-87328-231-4
ISBN (cloth) 978-0-87328-218-5

Library of Congress Cataloging-in-Publication Data

Lyons, Gary.
  Desert plants : a curator's introduction to the Huntington desert garden / Gary Lyons.
     p. cm.
  Includes bibliographical references and index.
  ISBN 978-0-87328-231-4 (alk. paper)
  1. Desert plants--California--San Marino. 2. Desert gardening--California--San Marino.
  3. Huntington Botanical Gardens. I. Title. II. Title: Curator's introduction to the
Huntington desert garden.
  SB427.5.L76 2007
  635.9'52507479493--dc22
                              2006101789

TABLE OF CONTENTS

OVERLEAF The Desert Garden contains more than
five thousand species of cacti and other succulents, some
of which are known for their bold geometric and
sculptural shapes, strong textures, and dazzling colors.

FOREWORD

THIS IS THE FIRST PUBLICATION by the Huntington on the Desert Garden since 1964, and thus has much ground to cover. As you might imagine, when a garden includes twelve acres of plants, rockery, and paths, has several thousand species to boast, and entails the life's work of many people, there are wonderful specimens to encounter, great stories to tell, and myriad lessons to learn.

You will discover that the Desert Garden inspires everyone who works at and visits the Huntington. It is not simply that this is a large garden with unique displays of great plant diversity. You do not merely visit the Desert Garden: you enter it, you are surrounded by and immersed in this wholly different, and at first sight, perhaps strange dreamscape. This garden takes you in and speaks to you with a fresh and compelling voice. Shape, form, movement, color, and texture have different meaning here. Plant life and presentation defy, and then re-construct your sense of what might be possible. The Desert Garden is a place that has been seen by over 20 million people in wonder and delight, a place of great meaning that I have toured with countless visitors, marveling at their own first discovery. It is the place that landscape architect Roberto Burle Marx called "the most extraordinary garden in the world." When you come to know his work, that statement takes exponential value.

The Desert Garden is about plants, plants with different habits from different habitats than the North Temperate, or even humid Tropical vegetation that fills our gardens and greenhouses. In this book, we cover as much botanical territory as possible in the pages available. However, there is so much more to see and learn, great reason for you to consider this book a beginning rather than an end in your conversation with these wonderful characters.

But a garden exists only as people can make it happen. Thus the Desert Garden embodies lives, the lives of many people who plant and garden, collect and study, propagate and nurture. The coming together of collections and display represents their work, dedication, and inspiration. It is clearly a garden loved by those who have built it, a garden that shares their passion for plants you may see as being over the top, green beings at their most diverse and expressive. The passion abides from generation to generation of staff and volunteers, and gives the Huntington the great opportunity to speak to you—the public—to tell you about the wonderful beauty and diversity of succulent plants, to advance stories of botany, ecology, and horticulture that we hope you will spend the rest of your life constructing and enjoying.

As an introduction to the stories behind these plants and this garden, as a reminder of a visit and encouragement for future forays, or as a resource for building your own collection and garden, we hope you find this book a favorite guide and resource.

Jim Folsom
Marge and Sherm Telleen Director
of the Botanical Gardens

A *Brief* History *of the* Huntington Desert Garden

IN LOS ANGELES AT THE turn of the twentieth century, railroad and real estate developer Henry Edwards Huntington (1850–1927) created one of the finest interurban railway systems ever built. He acquired large tracts of land for urban and suburban development and became the largest single landowner in Southern California at that time. He also was a collector without equal who assembled world-class collections of rare books and manuscripts, art, and plants.

In 1903 Huntington purchased the San Marino ranch, and with his foreman, William Hertrich, transformed it into a botanical garden of rare and exotic plants. One of their goals was to test plants for cultivation in Southern California gardens. The lily ponds were installed first, followed by the palm collection.

In 1907, Hertrich proposed the idea of establishing a cactus garden, known today as the Desert Garden. Other collections now include the Japanese, Rose, Shakespeare, Herb, Australian, and Subtropical gardens, a developing Chinese garden, and an internationally recognized camellia collection.

ABOVE   Henry E. Huntington
LEFT   The Huntington Desert Garden, c. 1916

WILLIAM HERTRICH, RANCH SUPERINTENDENT AND FOREMAN

IN THE LATE NINETEENTH and early twentieth centuries, many talented gardeners from Germany, Great Britain, and other European countries came to California to pursue opportunities in horticulture. One such person was Hertrich, who was born in Baden, Germany, in 1878; part of an agrarian family, he was educated in landscape gardening. In 1903, Hertrich headed to California, where two years later he was hired by George S. Patton Sr. to be the landscape gardener of Huntington's newly purchased San Marino ranch.

Hertrich went on to serve as the ranch's foreman and superintendent. With incredible energy and drive, he managed every aspect of ranch activity, from raising chickens and turtles to creating and caring for the landscape, guiding it to becoming one of the finest botanical gardens in North America. He designed and supervised the layout of the lily ponds, Palm Garden, Desert Garden, Rose Garden, and Japanese Garden, the scenic vistas from the residence, and most of the original tree and shrub plantings. After Huntington's death in 1927, the estate garden became a botanical garden that was open to the public, and Hertrich was appointed its first curator, a post he held until his retirement in 1948.

Hertrich's responsibilities in building the plant collections included accessioning, labeling, and recordkeeping. He also did extensive research, especially on ornamentals, fruiting trees, aloes, and cacti. His publications include the important three-volume work *Camellias in the Huntington Gardens* as well as *A Guide to the Desert Collections, Palms and Cycads*, and his personal reflections, *The Huntington Botanical Gardens, 1905–1949.*

Even after his retirement, Hertrich continued to work several days a week at his desk in the botanical department's library and was instrumental in keeping the gardens' development in line with Huntington's original vision. He also worked on describing and evaluating the numerous plants in the gardens based on his personal observations. Hertrich pursued Huntington's dream of evaluating plants for cultivation in Southern California, right up until his death in 1966.

TOP
William Hertrich, 1916
ABOVE LEFT
Henry E. Huntington,
c. 1922
RIGHT
William Hertrich with
Cereus grandicostatus,
c. 1940

CACTI IN THE SOUTHERN CALIFORNIA LANDSCAPE

CACTUS GARDENS and cactus specimens were common sights in Southern California landscaping from the late nineteenth century to the 1920s. Formal plantings could be seen in neighborhood parks, public landscapes, resort hotels, as well as estate gardens and collections. Along with palm and orange trees, "hot weather plants" such as cacti constituted the Southern California look. Cacti and succulents earned this appellation because they needed little water and could go without it during the hot dry summers. Until 1913, Southern California only had access to groundwater and water from the Los Angeles River, making desert gardens all the more desirable.

White Park in Riverside, California, designed by landscape architect Franz Hosp around 1893, had what was recognized as the premier Southern California desert garden as well as the largest and finest cactus collection in the United States. In the late 1800s, such prickly displays, called "Arizona Gardens," presented a stylized view of the vegetation of the Southwest's thorny deserts. Many of the plants used in these gardens came from Mexico and South America, whereas most of the plants used in landscaping came from a lively trade of specimens from local deserts.

ABOVE RIGHT   Reservoir below Desert Garden, 1909;
residence is under construction in background at left
RIGHT   White Park in Riverside, California, 1931

THE DESERT GARDEN'S BEGINNINGS

THE IDEA TO create the Desert Garden came from Hertrich, who had grown cacti in his windowsill garden in Germany. In spring 1907, he approached Huntington with a proposal for a cactus garden. Huntington initially winced at Hertrich's plan, for he recalled an encounter with some prickly pears that he had backed into while he was a field supervisor for the Southern Pacific Railroad. But later in the year, Huntington relented and allowed him to construct a trial garden. Hertrich had the foresight to situate the garden on a south-facing slope, which provided warmth, maximum exposure to the sun, and adequate drainage. He scoured Southern California nurseries—many of them holding large stocks of cacti—for specimens of all types and sizes, mostly Southwest desert natives. At that time, there was a great deal of trade in cacti collected throughout the Southwest and down into central Mexico. When the garden was finished in 1908, a few neatly laid out beds with narrow dirt paths were fringed with smooth, water-polished, pale-gray granite obtained from nearby arroyos. Some cacti, such as *Cephalocereus senilis*, were planted with a geometric neatness.

ABOVE
Golden barrel cacti
(*Echinocactus grusonii*) in the Desert Garden nursery, 1925
RIGHT 1912 view of garden with paths edged with river rock and Huntington residence in background

Hertrich's prickly garden aroused little enthusiasm from Huntington until his acquaintances began calling at the ranch to admire not the priceless art treasures and rare books, but rather the novel and eye-catching cactus collection. As a result, Huntington authorized Hertrich to collect and import more cacti and succulents. In 1908, a huge consignment of Arizona cacti arrived, including a carload of saguaros. In 1912, Hertrich traveled to Mexico and returned with a massive collection of succulents. The specimens added that year included golden barrel cacti, pincushions, old man cacti covered in white hair, century plants, tree yuccas, cerei, and finally aloes and euphorbias. By then, the garden had been enlarged to three acres, its appearance matching the stiffness and symmetry that characterized other estate cactus gardens at that time. The tone was still native and dominated by the many Mojave and Sonoran desert cacti.

TOP   Desert Garden, 1910
ABOVE   A car decorated with desert plants for an early Pasadena Tournament of Roses Parade

Much of the original Desert Garden planting was lost in a 1913 freeze. Many of the specimen cacti died because they were incompatible with coastal Southern California's Mediterranean climate. Meanwhile, the surviving aloes, cacti, agaves, and yuccas thrived. The hillside garden became packed with plants.

Relief came in 1925, with an expansion that doubled the size of the Desert Garden. Huntington decided to fill in the reservoir below the garden and sell some of his orange groves to the south. Workers carefully boxed, wired, and padded huge specimens of cerei, yuccas, beaucarneas, and agaves and rolled them to the new addition. Most of the small beds were formed, and key plantings of aloe, cereus, and yucca were laid out to define them.

In this new area, Hertrich constructed numerous, slightly elevated, display beds based on a wagon-wheel plan: a round bed, which still exists in the lower Desert Garden, with paths radiating out from the central axis. In this formal layout, he used arroyo granite to define a network of narrow dirt paths. At the corners of the geometric-shaped beds, he placed large boxed cereus specimens such as *C. peruvianus* 'Monstrose' and *C. dayamii*, which he had moved down the hill on boards and rollers. The largest specimens seen today in the lower Desert Garden are remnants of these original plantings. Today most are well over 100 years old.

C. xanthocarpus, acquired in 1912, is the oldest cactus in the garden, dating back to the 1880s. Though it is at the end of its life span, it will continue to exist through vegetative propagation. To what age cerei, and cacti in general, live in the wild, is unknown. Saguaros live 120 to 160 years, but there are few cacti that live that long.

C. xanthocarpus is a perfect example of the need to conserve biodiversity by propagating current holdings for the enjoyment of future generations. Even though it is perfectly suited as a landscape plant for Southern California gardens, the Huntington's dying specimen may be the only known example in cultivation.

TOP Workers moving *Cereus dayamii*
ABOVE *C. xanthocarpus* in its prime in the 1970s

THE TRANSITION FROM ESTATE
TO PUBLIC BOTANICAL GARDEN

AFTER THE DEATH OF HUNTINGTON in 1927, substantial modifications were made to the private estate to create an artfully landscaped botanical garden for public viewing. From 1929 to 1931, the Desert Garden was completely transformed by the construction of a broad central path and rockery over 900 feet long. This was the Desert Garden's greatest facelift, representing a break from the formalism found in parts of the estate garden landscape. It required the excavation of thousands of cubic yards of soil and the construction of complex rockeries. A railroad siding was built in the lower Desert Garden to bring in hundreds of tons of volcanic rock called scoria. To this day, the exact source of the scoria is unknown; it may have come from the Owens Valley in eastern California or from somewhere in Arizona. For at least two years, dozens of workers unloaded the rock from railroad cars, reloaded it onto horse-drawn sleds, and dragged it into the garden. Hertrich personally positioned each stone. Photos taken immediately following the installation suggest that some of Hertrich's background in formalism crept into this new display, which

still survives along portions of the garden's central path. It is most conspicuous in the pincushion rockery. Here one can see that the rockeries were constructed as a series of backfilled cells, like a beehive, and unified by the scoria. Initially, cacti were planted in the center of each cell, giving the display an even more unnatural appearance. Fortunately for the accomplishment of a naturalistic design, the plants did not stay on center, and many became nestled among rocks, just as they would have in the wild.

OPPOSITE ABOVE   Central path, 1930
OPPOSITE BELOW   *Neobuxbaumia polylopha*, 1925;
Dasylirion longissimum, 1925; *Cereus glaucus*, c. 1935
ABOVE   Central path in lower Desert Garden, c. 1932
RIGHT   William Hertrich in
front of *Cereus huntingtonianus*, c. 1945

HUNTINGTON INSTILLED IN HERTRICH that the primary purpose of the Desert Garden was to test economic and ornamental plants to see if they were suitable for the Mediterranean-like climate of Southern California. Early on, the Huntington and other estate gardens caught the attention of research botanists; plant explorers; the U.S. Department of Agriculture (USDA); botanical gardens in Europe, South Africa, and Mexico; repositories; and research collections. These important contacts contributed plants that remain important components of the Desert Garden: for example, the collections of aloes, agaves, yuccas, euphorbias, and cacti—particularly cereus and opuntia. In this early era, the Huntington received collections of opuntia from David Griffiths, a U.S. government botanist with the USDA. Before 1920, the garden also received plants from N. L. Britton and J. N. Rose, who were compiling *The Cactaceae* (1919–23), then the most authoritative monograph on the cactus family.

The Desert Garden fell on hard times shortly after the grounds opened to the public. During the Great Depression and World War II, the Huntington had a fifteen- to twenty-year hiatus in grounds maintenance. During this period, only a small portion of the Desert Garden remained open to the public.

Meanwhile, other botanical gardens, researchers, and plant collectors—particularly those affiliated with the Cactus and Succulent Society of America, founded in 1929—continued to share plants and seeds with the Huntington. Many large collections and estate gardens were offered to the institution. Some of these did not make an appearance in the public gardens; they were planted out of public view. Hertrich acquired many new agaves and aloes from the then-famous Hanbury Botanic Gardens in La Mortola, on the Italian Riviera. He kept these collections in a large glasshouse adjacent to the offices east of the library and where the entrance pavilion now stands. In the 1940s and 1950s, important collections of yucca and agave were planted in the lower garden. Some of the yuccas were used by Susan Delano McKelvey to describe the species in her *Yuccas of the Southwestern United States* (1938). Howard Scott Gentry, a USDA botanist, provided numerous agaves that still dominate much of the landscape. Gentry was one of the world's foremost authorities on agaves, and his fieldwork in Mexico greatly augmented the Huntington's displays. His research resulted in the monograph *Agaves of Continental North America*, first published in 1982 and now a classic. A few species, such as *A. parryi* var. *truncata* and *A. mapisaga* var. *lisa*—still growing in the lower garden—were described in that monograph.

William Hertrich with flowering *Agave mapisaga* var. *lisa*, 1959

A NEW START FOR THE DESERT GARDEN

IN 1962, MYRON KIMNACH, a succulent specialist from the University of California at Berkeley Botanical Garden, became superintendent of the gardens. Kimnach revived the Desert Garden survey that had been conducted annually during the Hertrich era. Under his tenure, the main objectives for the Desert Garden became recordkeeping, building up the botanical department's reference library, conducting garden surveys, labeling accurately, introducing plants, and relandscaping. Renovation of the greenhouses, additions to the collections, and new propagating facilities for succulents were other important projects.

Kimnach also reopened channels of communication and exchange with botanical gardens and collectors throughout the world. Three years after his arrival, the renovation and relandscaping of the upper Desert Garden began. This area had once been part of Hertrich's test plots for aloe and cereus hybrids as well as the Desert Garden nursery. In 1966 it was opened as the Africa section. Many of the plants that Hertrich grew and studied were aloes, and they now form the foundation of one of the largest aloe collections outside of Africa. In addition to aloes, this section includes caudiciform and geophytic succulents, ice plants, euphorbias, crassulas, and senecios. A program of plant exploration and introduction begun in 1966 greatly benefited the Desert Garden and the subtropical collections. Destinations for such expeditions included Mexico, South America, South Africa, and Madagascar.

LEFT The pincushion cacti in
their prime, 1960
BELOW Lower garden, c. 1960

Annual May plant sales began in 1975 to help distribute excess plant material to the public, finance collecting trips to Mexico, and purchase books for the botanical library. A major feature of the sale was—and is—its enormous selection of succulents. Initially, these were propagated from Desert Garden material.

In 1972, the Sonoran display in the lower garden was landscaped with cacti and other succulents native to northern Mexico and the Southwest United States, and it includes a substantial collection of documented barrel cacti (ferocactus). The Baja bed was installed in 1981; its ferocity of design may cause shock and awe for those who are not acquainted with well-armed spiny and thorny succulents such as the creeping devil cactus. The succulents of Baja display the struggle for survival in its most menacing form.

The Baja bed is dominated by a grove of boojum trees that were first brought to the Huntington about 1930 by a pioneering Southern California collector, Howard Gates. Known at the time as "Mr. Cactus," Gates was the first person to drive an auto the full length of Baja California in search of cacti. He also supplied the Huntington with its first specimen of *Yucca valida*, a central Baja relative of *Y. filifera*, the giant tree yucca found in central Mexico. The original plant still exists below the Heritage Walk and covers an entire bed.

TOP *Fouquieria columnaris* (boojum) in leaf
LEFT *Yucca valida*
OPPOSITE *Stenocereus eruca*, foreground, tree-like
F. columnaris, center

THE DESERT GARDEN CONSERVATORY

A LARGE, CUSTOM-BUILT glasshouse opened to the public in 1984 as the Desert Garden Conservatory. Located at the extreme north end of the African section, it is a teaching greenhouse with some 2,000 plants arranged in a classical taxonomic format. There is a basic division between Old and New World succulent plant families, which are organized further by genus, and where possible, by species. Visitors can see examples of rare and difficult-to-grow plants. Most of the plants cannot be successfully grown outdoors because of their specialized habitat. The collections give the visitor and student the opportunity to compare and contrast survival strategies in succulents.

ABOVE RIGHT
Welwitschia mirabilis cones
ABOVE
Crassula barklyi
RIGHT
W. mirabilis, Melocactus conoideus, and *Uebelmannia pectinifera* var. *multicostata*

RIGHT *Argyroderma congregatum,*
Astrophytum asterias 'Super Kabuto'

RIGHT *Conophytum, Ariocarpus agavoides*
and *A. kotschoubeyanus*

THE HERITAGE WALK

In 2003, a two-acre section of the Desert Garden was renovated and landscaped. This is the Heritage Walk, in which sixty tons of water-worn arroyo granite boulders harmonize with the garden's original layout.

The Desert Garden was constructed during the Craftsman era and the golden age of Southern California estate gardening, and this new section closely resembles the desertscape that was once enjoyed by Mr. Huntington. At that time, it was common to see driveways and flower beds lined with native arroyo granite river rock. The landscape stone used in Huntington's time may have been gathered on the ranch and employed by Hertrich to outline small beds. Most of the plants in this Heritage Walk represent materials that were used in Southern California gardens between 1880 and 1930. The one exception is the massive clumps of unusual terrestrial bromeliads, particularly puya, from T. Harper Goodspeed's expedition to the Andes. Goodspeed wrote about his plant-collecting adventures and research in his book *Plant Hunters in the Andes* (1941), now a classic. These drab semi-succulents produce spectacular flowers from late March to May. Many landscape painters and photographers are amazed at the intense, luminescent viridian, chartreuse, and violet hues of the blossoms that fill the six-foot stalks.

Beginning in mid-December and extending into January, visitors can view a sensational floral display of *Aloe arborescens*, one of the first aloes to be introduced to Southern California gardens. *A. ×principis*, a naturally occurring hybrid of *A. arborescens* and *A. ferox*, also flowering, is part of the display that can be seen from the north end of the Heritage Walk. Here also are some of the cerei that Hertrich and his crew boxed and moved from the hill in 1925. Still thriving, they flower from July to September.

Hertrich's love of succulent plants was clearly revealed in the accession catalogue, begun in 1932, which assigns a name, number, and source for each new plant. For this project he hired Eric Walther, a succulent enthusiast who went on to become one of the world's foremost authorities on echeveria and the director of San Francisco's Strybing Arboretum in Golden Gate Park. Not surprisingly, the Desert Garden material was chosen as the first to be accessioned. *Agave celsii* var. *albicans*, then called *A. albicans*, was given the first entry in the catalogue; this plant can still be seen on the east side of Heritage Walk.

The Heritage Walk reflects how much of the Desert Garden's landscape, beauty, and mystery are in reality the products of survival. This century-old garden includes survivors that have endured at least five major freezes, one hurricane, temperatures well over 110 degrees Fahrenheit, as well as the exigencies of two world wars and the Great Depression. In 1949, a snowstorm accompanied by one of Southern California's most serious freezes destroyed or damaged nearly 70 percent of the Desert Garden.

OPPOSITE LEFT   Heritage Walk marker
OPPOSITE TOP   *Sempervivum calcareum* 'Houseleek'
ABOVE   Heritage Walk, with steps built by
William Hertrich in 1907
RIGHT   Cactus fence (*Pachycereus marginatus*)

THE GARDEN'S CORE COLLECTIONS

Euphorbia magnicapsula in center, *E. coerulescens*
in background, and *E. echinus* in foreground right
Flowering *Yucca rigida* in center, *Agave* 'Boutin Blue'
in left foreground, and flowering lampranthus to right

THE DESERT GARDEN is more than a landscape display. Some call it a green treasure, a botanical ark, a prickly encyclopedia, another planet, a Garden of Eden, or a coral garden. Its significant collections of succulents are known as core collections, and they comprise the superstructure around which the garden is built. The core collections also define the garden's landscape, forming its backbone. They are well represented in the garden and include the following families: agave and yucca (Agavaceae), aloe (Aloaceae), puya (Bromeliaceae), cactus (Cactaceae), and succulent spurge (Euphorbiaceae). Many displays in the garden include combinations of agave, aloe, beaucarnea, cereus, echinocactus, hechtia, puya, euphorbia, mammillaria, ferocactus, borzicactus, echinopsis, and nolina.

Throughout the garden are many plantscapes organized somewhat by country, but because the pursuit of aesthetic beauty is the prevailing concept, this emphasis—the African section excepted—does not dominate the design. Many of the plants are grown from seeds or cuttings, or actual plants, collected in the wild. The earlier collections came from field botanists and specialists such as Joseph Nelson Rose, Curt Backeberg, Gilbert W. Reynolds, Howard Scott Gentry, and many others, including dedicated Huntington staff.

OPPOSITE   Cacti in pincushion rockery
TOP   Aloes in winter, Heritage Walk
ABOVE   *Puya venusta*

Desert Plants
of the Old World

THE AFRICAN SECTION OF the Desert Garden includes a heated bed consisting mostly of plants from Madagascar. Sometimes called the "Red Isle" and thought to be a remnant of the ancient supercontinent Gondwanaland, Madagascar is home to some of the world's most endangered flora. The garden's display includes large specimens, rarely seen in cultivation, of the didieria family (Didieriaceae), a group of spiny ocotillo-like succulents that grow in the thorn forests on the southwestern part of the island. The spiny *Alluaudia procera* and didieria forests are home to some of Madagascar's curious lemurs. Oddly, the lemurs are well adapted to arboreal life among the branches of these thorny trees. Some authorities consider the didieria family to be Old World cacti, for they may share a common ancestry.

LEFT   Dramatic display of *Aloe*
'William Hertrich,' 1970
TOP   *Alluaudia procera* stem and leaves
ABOVE   *Didierea trollii*

THE ALOE FAMILY

AT THE HUNTINGTON, visitors can see one of the largest aloe collections in the world—nearly 250 species, with everything from *Aloe albiflora* to *A. zebrina*. The aloes vary in size, from the tiny *A. descoingsii* of Madagascar, seen in the Desert Conservatory, to subtropical tree aloes such as *A. bainesii* that grow to sixty feet and more. Most species are of medium size and are solitary to shrubby. Some form enormous landscape shrubs, such as *A. ×principis* and *A. arborescens*, major sources of early winter garden color. Some aloes are jewels worth looking at in and out of flower—for example, *A. camperi* from Eritrea and Ethiopia and *A. dorotheae* of Tanzania, clump-formers with exotic, rich reddish-bronze leaves and graceful, creamy-white marginal teeth.

Aloes are Old World leaf succulents, with most garden species native to South Africa but distributed into east Africa, Madagascar, and southern Arabia. The word aloe is derived from the Hebrew "allal," meaning "bitter," or the Arabic "alloch." Aloes belong to the aloe family (Aloaceae), although some taxonomists prefer to list them in the asphodel family (Asphodelaceae). Their use in gardening and landscaping in Southern California dates only from the end of the nineteenth century.

ABOVE *Aloe descoingsii*
RIGHT *A. camperi, A. dorotheae,* and *A. suzanne* in fruit

ABOVE *Aloe bainesii* and *A. ciliaris*
at center, planted in the 1950s
RIGHT *A. hildebrandtii*

Aloe andongensis

Aloes form rosettes of thick, fleshy leaves that, when cut, release a free-flowing yellowish juice with a mucilaginous consistency. Their three-part flowers are tubular and borne on prominent stalks, with the tall *Aloe candelabrum*, *A. ferox*, and *A. spectabilis* being the showiest examples. On each flower petal are three thin green lines, called "honey guides," that direct insects into the flower's copious nectar supply. The flowers are colorful: pink, coral, and crimson, and sometimes yellow and even white, as in the diminutive *A. albiflora*. Their flowering season extends from October through March.

CLOCKWISE FROM TOP LEFT
Aloe ferox hybrid, *A. candelabrum*, *A. comptonii*,
and *A. arborescens*

Most aloes are prickly leaved, their thorns usually yellow or brownish in color. Commonly, the prickles are arranged along the margins and are very prominent in some species such as *A. melanacantha*, from the southwest Namibian desert. In drought, its leaves curve over the top of the plant with an armature of black prickles, protecting and shading the sensitive and juicy growth tip.

Aloes, especially *A. vera*, are known for the medicinal qualities of their leaf sap. In fact, the aloe was the earliest succulent to be documented. A Sumerian tablet records the use of aloes in the Middle East as early as 1450 B.C.E., and centuries later it was one of the plants that the Franciscan missionaries brought to Southern California.

There are two distinct forms of the medicinal aloe: one a small, shiny-leaved form with coral flowers; the other, larger, with paler leaves and bright yellow flowers. The original localities of both kinds are unknown, but the smaller form is thought to have come from the Red Sea coast and been carried by caravan traders into the Mediterranean region. The larger Barbados aloe, the form introduced to the New World by the mission fathers and regarded by early herbalists as the best for veterinary medicine, is thought to be from either the Ethiopian highlands or from the frankincense region of southern Arabia. This is the form still grown commercially today.

In the nineteenth century, the small *A. vera* was described as *A. vera* var. *chinensis* because it was thought to be native to China—far beyond the natural range of the genus. Actually, Arab and Indian traders alleged that many commodities came from distant China—a ruse to conceal their sources from outsiders. In the 1960s, a new aloe species was introduced to cultivation; it had been collected at Massawa, Eritrea, an ancient Red Sea trade depot near the Indian Ocean where for centuries caravan traders had met sea traders. The aloe was named *A. massawana*, and when it flowered, only the slightest differences between it and the so-called China form were noted. Many herbalists regard the China form of *A. vera* as the best for treating minor cuts, bruises, and burns.

One curious specimen is *A. dichotoma*, the quiver tree, which has grown along Palm Garden Drive in the upper garden since 1932. The tree has branches occurring in pairs and a huge, thick trunk of decorative peeling bark. It is native to southwest Africa, and its crown glows with bright yellow flowers from October to November. Its name refers to the early Bushman practice of hollowing out its stubby branches to make arrow quivers. The flowers are a delicacy for baboons, but the plant at the Huntington only attracts photographers and hummingbirds. *A. ramosissima*, a close ally of *A. dichotoma* (and of *A. bainesii*), also has branches occurring in pairs. It is a sculpture-like shrub with short, finger-like leaves and flowers nearly identical to those of its tree-like relative.

The tall, single-rosette aloes in the Africa section are *A. ferox*, *A. marlothii*, and *A. spectabilis*. In late January to early March, they have elegant candelabra-like clusters of flowers. *A. spectabilis* has pleasantly contrasting reddish buds and yellow to orange flowers—a spectacular show

TOP *Aloe vera* (*A. barbadensis*)
ABOVE Thorns on *A. spectabilis* hybrid

TOP *A. dichotoma*
ABOVE Fleshy stalks of *A. vera*

that attracts pollinators. In Africa, the primary aloe pollinator is the malachite sunbird, but in Southern California, the pollinators are tiny hummingbirds. *A. spectabilis* grows to twenty feet. These tall, solitary aloes occasionally fall to the ground after a soaking rain, but the loss is only one of height, for gardeners cut the stem below the leaves and reroot them like a cutting.

A. 'William Hertrich' is a hybrid that was developed by Hertrich in the 1920s and 1930s. Its parentage is uncertain, but it could be a cross between *A. arborescens* and *A. pretoriensis*. Its coral red flowers appear in four- to eight-foot-tall clusters.

One of the strangest aloes, one that could have been taken from a Seussian landscape, is the fan aloe, *A. plicatilis*, native to moist regions of the Cape Province. It has an opposite arrangement of leaves, with each one stacked directly over the other—a rare phenomenon in the plant kingdom. It is a slow-growing shrub with spikes of coral red flowers in March.

Several specimens that survived in Hertrich's test plots now have a stately presence in the African section. One of his most successful crosses has a single rosette and is a repeat bloomer, with golden yellow flowers on stalks up

to six feet tall. The author has chosen to call them *A.* 'Henry Huntington' (see page 3).

Two more members of the aloe family should be noted: haworthia and gasteria. Both being native to South Africa, they are suitable for Mediterranean-climate gardens and are popular among collectors. The haworthia, named for Adrian Hardy Haworth, an early-nineteenth-century succulent collector and botanist, consists of small, usually clustering, rosettes of succulent leaves. Some species are windowed succulents—that is, light filters through the leaf tip, the only part of the leaf exposed to light, to photosynthetic tissue buried within the leaf. Two species in the Desert Garden Conservatory, *H. truncata* and *H. truncata* var. *maughanii*, possess this feature as well as some species growing in the garden. Haworthia flowers are quite small, tubular, and white, and are borne on delicate stalks or spikes. In the garden these plants are tucked among rocks in shaded areas.

Gasteria is similar to haworthia, but has an asymmetrical leaf arrangement and tolerates light shade, even full sun. Gasteria translates literally as "stomach flower," a reference to the swollen external part of the flower. Its flowers are pink and quite showy.

ABOVE *Aloe* 'William Hertrich' LEFT *Haworthia truncata*

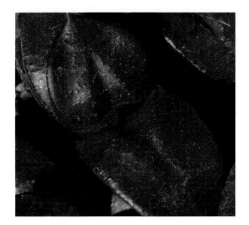

LEFT *Gasteria natida* var. *armstrongii*

EUPHORBIAS

THE SUCCULENT SPURGES (the word spurge is derived from *expurgare*, which means to purge, cleanse, or purify) are important components of the Desert Garden landscape and the Conservatory collection. Their globular and columnar shapes may cause visitors to mistake them for cacti. However, beyond their general shape, euphorbias bear no relation to the cactus family. The primary difference, apart from their whitish, caustic leaf sap, is in the floral and spine structures. The floral structure has, as observed in the Madagascan crown of thorns (*E. milii*), what appear to be flowers with red petals. In the center of the "flower" are tiny clusters of stamens and a stigma. These tiny clusters of male and female parts actually are the flowers; there are no petals. What look like red "petals" are called bracts, or petaloid bracts. These are outgrowths of the receptacle that encloses the individual tiny flowers. The entire structure is called a cyathium.

In other euphorbia species, such as the milk barrel (*E. horrida*), the cyathium is borne on a stout stalk, or peduncle; when the flower or fruit falls away, it dries to become a spine. In the cow's horn euphorbia (*E. grandicornis*) and in many of the South African species, one sees a different sort of spine. These arise at opposite sides of the developing flowers and are modified leaf parts called stipules; hence, they are called stipular spines. A third type of epidermal spine is found in many Madagascan species, readily seen in *E. milii* var. *hislopii*. These are irregularly shaped spines of various sizes and shapes that have no connection to the flowers or the leaf.

TOP *Euphorbia cooperi*
ABOVE *E.* 'Apache Red'
RIGHT *E. milii* hybrid,
E. horrida (showing unripe, "explosive" seed capsules), and *E. grandicornis*
OPPOSITE *E. xantii* flowers with the columnar pipe organ cactus, *Pachycereus marginatus*

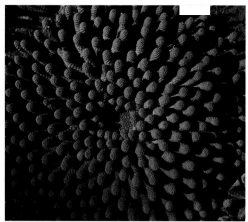

Euphorbia seeds are borne in small dry capsules that explode with a pop, propelling the seed away from the plant. The Desert Garden once contained an enormous *E. grandidens*, a treelike species from South Africa. When its thousands of seed capsules ripened, it sounded like the snap, crackle, and pop of rice breakfast cereal.

Most of the more than 500 euphorbia species are native to Africa (including the Canary Islands and Madagascar), the southern Middle East, and western India. Approximately 200 of these are in the Desert Garden and the Desert Conservatory. Among the earliest species known to the ancient Mediterranean world are *E. officinarum* from Morocco and *E. antiquorum* from southern Iraq and India.

Euphorbias were among the earliest succulents known to medicine, as their juice had many medical applications, most with very dangerous and unpleasant side effects. They were primarily used for their milk latex, which made a powerful purgative. Both Hippocrates and Theophrastus mention it and warn that if the juice gets in the eyes, the person can be blinded. In many parts of the world, it is still used as a purgative, as a treatment for skin lesions, and as a poison for arrows. This last usage is why we treat the succulent euphorbias with great care and caution, and why visitors should avoid touching or brushing against the plants. In spite of their negative attributes, the succulent euphorbias are popular in subtropical gardens and landscaping as well as among collectors.

ABOVE *Euphorbia atrispina, E. esculenta*
RIGHT *E. pseudocactus, E. lambii*

The euphorbia was given its name some 2,000 years ago by King Juba II of Mauritania to honor (or humiliate) his corpulent physician, Euphorbus. The euphorbia in Mauritania was called *euphorbion*, and today is better known as *E. officinarum*.

The Desert Conservatory is the best place to observe the many growth forms of euphorbia. Many produce true leaves, particularly those from Madagascar. The garden has several large specimens of tree species, particularly *E. ingens* and similar species from the savanna regions of southern and eastern Africa. These are subtropical, even tropical species, and prefer the warmest parts of the garden's African section. The Canary Islands offer curious leafy semisucculent shrubs like *E. lambii*, resembling in miniature the dichotomous branching habit of the dragon tree, which can be seen in the lower garden.

RIGHT *E. ingens*

THE CRASSULA FAMILY

THE CRASSULA FAMILY, Crassulaceae, consists of some three dozen genera of succulents native to both hemispheres of the Old and New Worlds (see page 62 for New World Crassulas). Most of the garden's Old World crassulas are native to South Africa, the Canary Islands, and Madagascar. Collectively, the crassulaceae include some of the most common and most colorful soft succulents for gardens, patios, or windows. Most are leaf succulents and propagate easily, and their distinguishing features include tiny, dust-like seeds and an equal number of floral parts—that is, they have the same number of stamens, carpels, sepals, and petals. The soft leaves are arranged spirally, or in rosettes, at opposite or right angles. The prominent structure bearing the flowers develops either as an extension of the shoot tip or from below it.

The genus *Crassula* comprises the largest African group, with about 300 species found mostly in South Africa. The showiest species in the garden is *C. perfoliata* var. *falcata*, an old-timer to cultivation that offers a flashy show of brilliant red flowers in August and September.

In contrast, the thick-trunked and fleshy jade tree, *C. ovata* ssp. *ovata*, along with its numerous cultivars and forms, has a definite softening or calming effect. The finest flowering specimens are just above the entrance to the garden's central walk and in the ground cover test bed across from the lily ponds; they are frosted from late October to December with masses of pinkish-white blossoms. With just the right amount of light frost, the flowers will darken in color.

ABOVE *Aeonium* 'Velour'
RIGHT *Crassula ovata* ssp. *ovata* (jade plant), flowering in December

Crassula perfoliata var. *falcata*

Kalanchoe. A closer inspection of the leaves of some kalanchoe species, like *K. delagoensis*, reveals a marvelous form of vegetative propagation: the production of an army of tiny rooted plantlets along each leaf edge and leaf tip. During dry spells, the plantlets readily detach, root, and grow wherever they touch the earth.

Aeonium. The steep, rocky slopes of the Canary Islands form the principal habitat of most of the forty-plus species and varieties of the genus *Aeonium*, well represented throughout the garden. The name aeonium means "eternal" or "ever-living," referring to the plant's drought-resistant properties. It is a woody-stemmed, rosette-forming succulent closely related to the Old World sempervivums and sedums. At one time they were called sempervivums, which also translates as "ever living."

Aeoniums typically have woody stems terminating in compact rosettes or spatula- or strap-shaped succulent leaves. They are fall- and winter-growing and remain dormant in summer. The large, many-flowered, pyramid-shaped clusters of yellow, white, or pink flowers emerge as an extension of the growth tip. In hot, dry summers, the rosettes contract, the outer ones wither and die, and all growth ceases. Many kinds appear more dead than alive during this dormant phase.

Aeoniums vary in size, from the diminutive subshrub, *A. sedifolium*, to the imposing *A. undulatum*, which grows up to six feet tall. In the Conservatory one finds the oddest species, *A. tabulaeforme*, a compact, saucer-like rosette of up to 200 leaves. First introduced to European gardens in 1696, this species is seldom seen in gardens today because it is difficult to grow, unless in a pot. It rarely reproduces, and lives four to six years before it flowers—then dies.

Bushy aeoniums are common in cultivation in Southern California, and are useful for their softening effect. They are easy to grow, withstand over-watering, and recover effortlessly from light frosts. *A. decorum*, *A. castello-paive*, and *A. haworthii* are all small shrubs.

In all aeoniums, the stem that flowers dies, and shrubby species sometimes flower themselves to pieces and have to be replanted after a few years. Beginning in October, the non-flowering shoots are removed and planted as cuttings. In a few weeks, with light waterings, they take root.

A. undulatum is the largest aeonium in the garden, forming a giant rosette of long, bright-green leaves with undulating margins. The plant branches only at the base and is useful for its height in plantings of succulents. It puts on a spectacular wintertime floral show as the long, slender stems are transformed into fountains of bright yellow flowers.

Several years ago, a deep purple–leaved sport of *A. arboreum* named 'Zwartkop' appeared in a Dutch nursery, and it now forms some of the most dramatic succulent displays in the garden. It thrives in full sun, and its dark color is enhanced if it is slightly underwatered. Fine displays of 'Zwartkop' and a new hybrid, *A.* 'Voodoo,' make striking contrast plantings at the upper garden entrance and along the road between the Desert and Palm gardens.

TOP   *Kalanchoe marmorata*
ABOVE   *K. thrysiflora*

TOP   *Aeonium arboreum* 'Voodoo' with flowering *Aloe vera*
ABOVE   *A. davidbramwellii*

Cotyledon and Tylecodon. The genus *Cotyledon* is appreciated for its soft, rounded shrubs with equally rounded leaves. Pendent and colorful bell-shaped flowers are borne from the stem tips. A little novelty succulent from South Africa's Cape Province, *C. tomentosa* ssp. *ladismithensis* is crowded with fuzzy, globular green leaves, each tipped with a purple blush.

Some of the caudiciform species of cotyledons—ones with tree-like swollen stems—have been placed in their own genus, *Tylecodon* (the name is an anagram of Cotyledon). Some types are sizeable, such as *T. paniculatus*, the butter tree, which is famous for its fat, gnarled trunk that can be cut with a dinner knife. The plant grows to nearly seven feet tall, in the parts of arid southwest Africa that have winter rainfall. *T. paniculatus* is named after its branched cluster of flowers, which emerges from the terminal growth but does not cause the death of the branch.

TOP *Cotyledon tomentosa* ssp. *ladismithensis*
ABOVE *Tylecodon paniculatus*

CYPHOSTEMMA
AND DIOSCOREA

TWO UNUSUAL CAUDICIFORMS found in the Africa section are *Cyphostemma juttae* and *Dioscorea elephantipes. C. juttae*, in the grape family, is from Namibia in southwest Africa and produces enormous fleshy leaves on stubby branches that drop off in the dry season. The dormant version of the plant looks like a tree trunk without a tree. The flowers are insignificant, and nicely arranged in flat-topped clusters, but the bright crimson fruits are grapelike in shape and slightly toxic. Other species are in the Desert Conservatory. August and September are the best months to see these grape relatives in full fruit and full leaf.

Elephant's foot (*D. elephantipes*), in the yam family, is one of the Desert Garden's most treasured specimens. Before the African section was developed, this particular plant grew, completely forgotten. Now some say this is the largest-known elephant's foot, even larger than those found in the wild in South Africa.

TOP RIGHT *Dioscorea elephantipes*
ABOVE AND RIGHT *Cyphostemma juttae*

Cyphostemma juttae, planted in 1980

Dioscorea elephantipes, growing in this location since 1931

THE DRAGON TREE

Dracaena draco

ONE OF THE largest dragon trees in cultivation in the United States is in the lower Desert Garden along Palm Garden Road. It dates to the end of the nineteenth century but is still just a baby. Dragon trees (*Dracaena draco*) were commonly used in Southern California landscaping, and many, many parks still have them. On its battered trunk can be seen encrustations of a red sap known as dragon's blood. This resin was used in Europe as an astringent, added to varnishes, and used as a marble stain as well as a treatment for gum disease. Italian violin-makers used it in the seventeenth and eighteenth centuries to stain wood. John Parkinson, in his 1640 herbal *Theatricum Botanicum*, stated: "The Glassiers use it much in their workes…to strike a crimson colour into glasse, for Windowes and the like."

STAPELIAS

STAPELIAS BELONG TO the milkweed family, and are generally difficult to grow in outdoor gardens in Southern California. However, they are well represented in the Desert Garden Conservatory, where they are not subject to the deleterious effects of cold, wet winters when they are dormant. The succulent stapeliads, comprising 1,000 species in sixty-one genera, possess one of the most highly specialized and complex floral systems and pollination strategies in the plant world. Stapeliads are called carrion flowers because they reek of putrid flesh when in full bloom and are therefore pollinated only by certain flies. The flies are attracted by the odor and lay their eggs in the center of the flower, where the odor is strongest. In the process, the fly's legs become coated with pollen. When it moves to another flower on a different plant and gets stuck again, the pollen left behind germinates and fertilizes the ovary. During the warm months in the garden, one can observe flies in action on *Stapelia gigantea*, the starfish flower, and *S. hirsuta*, the hairy starfish flower.

ABOVE   *Stapelia gigantea* flower bud
ABOVE RIGHT   Flies laying eggs on *S. gigantea*
RIGHT   Color variant of *S. gigantea*

ICE PLANTS

Species of the genus *Mesembryanthemum* (mesembs) have curiously sculpted, rock-like leaves, some of them drab and colorless. This drastically changes from winter to early spring, when ground covers transform the African display beds into eye-dazzling splashes of color. Most of the species open about noon, their color palette ranging from satiny white to yellow, pink, red, purple, and every shade in between (the word mesembryanthemum translates literally as "noonday flower plant"). They are called ice plants in reference to the conspicuous watery papillae, or hairs, covering the leaf surfaces of some species; these are especially obvious in the spinach-like annual herb *M. crystallinum*.

Mesembs are leaf succulents with leaves in pairs, in opposite rows, the new pair emerging from between the old pair at right angles. Of the family's 2,500 species and 122 genera (equal in size to the cactus family and nearly all of them from South Africa), most have flowers with numerous shimmering petals and petal-like structures that are modified stamens. The fruit is a dry capsule, except for the edible Hottentot fig, *Carpobrotus edulis*, a common ground cover in Southern California landscaping.

TOP *Ceroclamys pachyphylla*
ABOVE Flowering *Cheiridopsis*

Several mesembs are planted in rockeries in the African section, but the best flowering displays are found in the ground cover beds along Palm Garden Drive, which have *Faucaria, Pleiospilos, Cephalophyllum, Rhombophyllum, Cheiridopsis,* and *Lampranthus. Lithops, Conophytum,* and *Ophthalmophyllum*—all mimicry types—are in the Desert Conservatory.

In April or May, the lampranthus—which means "bright flower"—is in full bloom, with sparkling sheets of crimsons, yellows, pinks, and whites. The best garden displays are the deep-pink *L. amoenus* and *L. formosus* and the golden yellow *L. aurantiacus.*

TOP AND ABOVE   *Lampranthus*

SENECIOS, OR SUCCULENT SUNFLOWERS

THE GENUS *Senecio* belongs to the sunflower family. Admittedly, the flowers of most succulent senecios are not much to look at, but their flowers are compacted within a fleshy receptacle that looks like a single flower. As with euphorbias, the true flowers are small and insignificant, except for some species that have outer flowers with large showy petals.

Many senecios are scraggly herbs, and some are shrubs. Many of the species are used as ground covers and are bluish or gray-green. The leaves are covered with a thick, waxy substance that protects them from excess evaporation and gives the leaf a soft pastel effect. Some species, like *S. haworthii*, are covered with a white fuzz that makes for a charming garden plant; the main function of the covering is to insulate the leaves from water loss.

The blue-leaved senecios, *S. talinoides* ssp. *mandraliscae*, thought to come from Cape Province but possibly a hybrid, and *S. serpens* (*Kleinia repens*), definitely from the Cape, are abundantly planted for their cooling effect and to add a softening element in the historic section of the lower garden. *S. talinoides* ssp. *mandraliscae* is the better ground cover, with its rapid growth and larger leaves.

ABOVE *Senecio talinoides* ssp. *mandraliscae* and golden barrel cacti
OPPOSITE *S. talinoides* ssp. *mandraliscae* and *Drosanthemum bicolor*

Desert Plants
of the New World

THE EUROPEAN DISCOVERY OF the New World dramatically challenged and expanded knowledge of plant diversity and medicinal and economic plants. The Spanish physician Nicolás Monardes gave the following graphic account of his contact with a cactus: "One of the thornes that it hath did pricke mee. They [the spines] are strong as needles and did hurt me. It seemeth to be a strange hearbe" (*Joyfull Newes out of the Newe Founde Worlde*, 1568).

LEFT   Pincushion cactus nestle in red scoria, c. 1978
TOP   Puya flowers
ABOVE   *Ferocactus robustus*

NEW WORLD CRASSULAS

Echeveria, the most attractive group in the crassula family, contains over 150 species. Its distribution is concentrated in Mexico, extending south into Venezuela and Peru. The plants are small succulent herbs, solitary or clump forming; some are bushy, and all produce rosettes of symmetrically arranged leaves. The urn-shaped flowers are usually pinkish-red, some orange and yellow, and they are borne on single-branched stalks. Echeverias grow in rocky areas and on cliffs, ranging from an elevation of 9,000 feet down to mesquite grasslands at 1,500 feet. Most are found in pine-oak woodland, growing under shaded and cool conditions, which explains the difficulty they have in growing in hotter climates.

One of the Desert Garden's most colorful echeverias is *E. colorata* var. *brandtii*, named for Fred Brandt, a Huntington grounds superintendent who discovered it in 1968 during an expedition to Mexico. It is presumed to be extinct in nature, and now this one clone survives in the garden through horticultural propagation. There is a beautiful light green–leaved species in the Heritage Walk called *E. pallida*. It is one of the few large-leaved species that thrive in the Desert Garden.

ABOVE RIGHT, FROM TOP   *Echeveria agavoides* × *E. colorata*,
Echeveria colorata var. *brandtii*, and *E. pulvinata*
ABOVE LEFT   *E. imbricata*
OPPOSITE   *E. pallida*

CACTI

SOUTHERN CALIFORNIA PROVIDES an excellent climate for cactus species native to the western slopes of the Andes as well as dry grassland and thorn scrub regions of Brazil, Bolivia, Paraguay, and Uruguay. The word cactus is derived from *kaktos*, a Greek word meaning thistle. Christopher Columbus is reported to have brought specimens to Spain in 1496, following his second voyage to the New World.

As a plant family, cacti are clearly distinct from other groups and have one very important characteristic: they protect their thirst-quenching pulp from the thirsty and curious with an armature of sharp spines. Cactus spines differ from euphorbia thorns and prickles and those of other succulents in that they arise from a woolly structure called an areole. Areoles are clearly defined plant organs set upon ribs—as seen in the columnar cacti—or upon (and between) knobby protuberances known as tubercles, as seen in many globular cacti. Spines arise from the areoles, as do branches, flowers, and fruit. The areole protects the vital structures beneath the plant's surface so that they cannot be devoured by insects and other small animals.

ABOVE   Knobby protuberances on cactus
RIGHT   Spines set on ribs

Spines occur in various sizes, shapes, and colors: they can be needle-like and up to twelve inches long, or they can be hooked, as in many barrel cacti with their bristling spread of radial spines. They can also be hair-like, woolly, flat, papery, or barbed. In addition, some cacti have tiny dust-like spinelets called glochids that cause severe itching and inflammation. Besides providing protection, spines give some shade to the plant to reduce water loss.

Some cacti, like the columnar pilosocereus, produce so much wool from their areoles that the top of the stem is white and appears fluffy. This wool further protects the plant, its flowers, and its fruit from predators as well as intense heat and sunlight.

The flower is the most joyful feature of the cactus family: no other succulent plant group has blossoms so large, so spectacular, or of such an intense hue. April and May are the best months to see the sunbursts of cactus flowers. These blossoms are tubular or cup-shaped and have numerous petals that are very thin and fragile, and are covered with a translucent reflective sheen to convey color across miles of arid landscape.

ABOVE Cactus flowers are tubular and cup-shaped
RIGHT Needle-like spines, hook-like spines, and fluffy wool

Mexican pincushion cactus display includes the columnar
Neobuxbaumia euphorbioides at
top center and the globular golden barrel at center

Cacti are unsurpassed in their variety of shapes and sizes. They can be shrubby with true leaves and stalked flowers like the so-called primitive genus *Pereskia*, growing above the Mexican pincushion cactus display. There are also the spineless but well-camouflaged, rock-like ariocarpus in the Desert Conservatory, the forty-foot-tall candelabra-branched trees such as cereus and stenocereus, and even the pumpkin-shaped cacti, as in the golden barrel. A stroll through the garden reveals a tremendous multiplicity of form exceeded by no other family of succulents. On the east side of the central path are displays of globular, shrubby, and columnar cacti, all with colorful spring flowers.

The garden's most conspicuous South American cacti are the ceroids, the columnar or ribbed cacti, including: *Cereus, Cleistocactus, Echinopsis,* and *Borzicactus.* Not all species are columnar; many are in fact globular, yet ribbed, cereus. The cerei, with their powerful, columnar, tree-like forms, are the largest, and they dominate parts of the garden. Cereus, meaning a wax taper or candle, was first described in 1754 by Phillip Miller. The name is older, for the botanist Tabernaemontanus used it in 1625 in reference to *Cereus peruvianus.* A specimen of this species, identified by Joseph Nelson Rose, can be seen near the road separating the Desert and Palm gardens.

CLOCKWISE FROM ABOVE LEFT *Pereskia grandiflora, Cereus peruvianus reclinatus* var. *retroflexus,* and *Ariocarpus fissuratus* var. *lloydii*

Cerei have large, funnel-shaped white flowers with a conspicuous green tube along with large, smooth, edible fruit. Their delicate blossoms are nocturnal and lustrous white, sometimes with a pinkish midstripe. The plants make dramatic landscape specimens and excel as forceful background colonnades setting off smaller plants. Other genera that are similar to cereus are referred to collectively, along with cereus, as ceroids.

The best time to view the remarkable cereus blossoms is on an overcast morning in August or September. In October, the cereus fruits ripen and become pink to deep crimson (canary yellow in *C. peruvianus*), and their appearance and delicious taste earn them the well-deserved name "cactus apples."

Cerei often have a bluish cast that is most intense in the spectacular *Browningia hertlingiana* of Peru, seen near the upper Desert Garden entrance. Most grow into medium to large, densely branched trees, such as *C. dayamii* and *C. jamacaru*.

C. huntingtonianus is one of the few pink-flowered cerei. Located off the central path in the lower garden, it opens at night. Named in honor of Henry E. Huntington, it was first described in 1927. A probable relative is *C. grenadensis*, native to the Caribbean island of Grenada, a beautiful accent plant that grows slowly and for much of its life remains small but well structured and sculpturesque. Eventually it becomes a large shrub. Its name could refer to the fruit, for the pulp is an eye-catching, grenadine-like color.

TOP *Trichocereus thelegonus* flower, ripe cereus fruit
ABOVE *Cereus ortesii*

Massive specimens of monstrose, or monstrous, cerei are used as foundation plantings in many areas of the garden. Their bizarre appearance results from a mysterious growth anomaly that breaks up the symmetrical rib pattern into knobs and irregular segments, yet produces perfectly healthy growth. Many stems terminate irregularly in crests or fasciations—also without explanation. Chromosomal anomaly and disease damage to the growth tip are suggested causes of monstrose growth and fasciations. Such cresting also occurs in globular cacti and is much prized by collectors. The dominant representatives in the garden are *C. horribarbis* (the most robust) and *C. milesimus*.

TOP *Cereus huntingtonianus*
ABOVE Monstrose cereus, *C. horridus* var. *macrocarpus*

Cleistocactus strausii 'Wooly Torch'

Many of the shrubby elements in the South American cactus display are from the genus *Cleistocactus*. There are fifty species in this genus, one-third of which are in the garden. All are native to the dry regions of central Peru, Bolivia, Argentina, and Paraguay. Cleistocacti are slender-stemmed plants with many shallow ribs and short, needle-like spines. They form basally branching clumps or dense, sprawling thickets, and their thin stems easily distinguish them from cereus. The flowers are tubular and bright scarlet. "Cleistos" means closed, referring to the partial closing of the flowers that allows only for the protrusion of the stigma, or female part of the flower.

The finest cleistocacti in the garden are *C. strausii* and *C. hyalacanthus*, both forming handsome, erect-branched shrubs cloaked with snow-white to yellowish spines and hairlike bristles. This dense covering insulates the plant from intense heat and sunlight.

Trichocereus is related to two genera known as *Echinopsis* and *Lobivia*—both much smaller in size. A comparison of flowers and fruit of the three genera shows only minute differences, but the generic name signifies the presence of hairs on the buds, flower receptacles, and fruit. Today some botanists include cleistocactus, echinopsis, lobivia, and trichocereus in a single genus, *Echinopsis*. At least sixty *Trichocereus* species range from the drylands and deserts of Ecuador to Chile and Argentina.

CLOCKWISE FROM TOP LEFT
Echinopsis 'Fiesta Gold,' *E.* 'Volcanic Sunset,'
and *E. multiplex*

Most of the garden's larger trichocerei, such as Argentina's giant saguaro-like *T. pasacana*, are shrubby. *T. pasacana* grows to thirty feet and has the same massive candelabra habit as the Southwest native. Python-sized branches of *T. anglesii* snake along the ground in the lower garden opposite the Baja bed, an example of some of the more unusual design effects realized in the different growth habits of cacti.

The dry Andean region is home to the genus *Borzicactus*. Many of the species reveal differences, so much so that botanists place several in separate genera. *B. (Matucana) aurantiacus*, the most attractive of the globular types, is shiny green with rounded projections and elegant golden yellow spines. This Peruvian beauty has tubular, showy, golden-orange flowers.

The largest borzicacti are shrubby and columnar. The garden's finest is *B. samaipatanus*, named for the Bolivian village of Samaipatana, near where it was discovered. The flowers are bright scarlet and zygomorphic, a word that describes their unequal arrangement of petals. The upper petals remain straight and unexpanded to protect the stamens and their copious pollen. This positioning permits a thorough dusting of insects as they leave the flower and carry pollen to the next one. The most popular borzicacti are the old man of the Andes, *B. (Oreocereus) celsianus*, and the old woman of the Andes, *B. fossulatus*, which are characterized by thick stems with a dense covering of long white hairs. This protective covering gives the stems added protection from water loss and insulation from cold and heat.

ABOVE *Borzicactus samaipatanes* plant and flower
OPPOSITE Plantings include the tall *Trichocereus pasacana* at center, and the Arizona ironwood (*Olneya tesota*) in background

The cacti and other succulents of Mexico are unsurpassed for their variety of colors, shapes, and textures. Mexico's soils, mineralized volcanic and limestone formations, geography, and climate combine to make a setting for plant worlds of great beauty and dramatic contrast. The country's deep canyons, wooded hills, and impenetrable thorn forests conceal the greatest diversity and species concentration in the cactus, agave, and crassula families.

One interesting Mexican cactus to view is astrophytum ("star plant," referring to its starlike appearance). The best-known astrophytum is the spineless bishop's cap cactus (*A. myriostigma*), a low, nearly flat species with five or more broad ribs that looks a bit like a bishop's miter. Myriostigma means "covered with a myriad of little dots"; these protect the plant from water loss and provide some camouflage. The bishop's cap is conspicuous in the garden setting, but in the wild, its color and texture blend in with its native limestone habitat. *A. myriostigma*'s bright yellow flowers appear and reappear throughout late spring and summer. Another one to look for is the large, bold-angled species with golden spines. *A. ornatum*, named for the ornate arrangement of felt-like dots sprinkled over the plant surface.

TOP *Astrophytum myriostigma* (bishop's cap)
ABOVE *A. ornatum*

Numerous ferocactus grow well in the garden, as they tolerate the rainfall and mild weather. *F. robustus* from Puebla and Tehuacán in central Mexico is most attractive. In the wild, it forms enormous green mounds up to three feet high and nine feet across. The Desert Garden's specimens are smaller but still impressive. *F. glaucescens*, sometimes called the blue barrel, is one of the barrel cactus beauties with a blue-gray stem and a mantle of short, pale yellow spines. *F. macrodiscus*, named for its saucer-like appearance, has delightful candy-striped pink flowers.

LEFT   The pincushion rockery
in 1971
BELOW *Mammillaria compressa,*
M. longimamma, M. polythele
ssp. *polythele (M. tetracantha),*
and *Cephalocereus senilis*

Pilosocereus leucocephalus,
William Hertrich with
Neobuxbaumia scoparia

A rockery on the west side of the central path contains an interesting display of pincushion cacti. These small, globular cacti belong to the genus *Mammillaria*; containing 250 species, it is one of the largest genera in the cactus family. First described in 1812 by the eminent English botanist Adrian Hardy Haworth, the genus lacks ribs but is covered with spiraling rows of small nodules called tubercles. Mammillarias are found throughout the Northern Hemisphere, ranging from the deserts of the Southwest to Colombia, Venezuela, and the West Indies, and concentrated in Mexico. *M. compressa* and *M. geminispina* have grown for years in the rockery; they start flowering in early January.

The pincushion rockery is framed and backed by several kinds of columnar cacti, particularly *Pilosocereus*, *Cephalocereus*, and the closely related but rarely seen genus, *Neobuxbaumia*. Pilosocerei are woolly, bluish-stemmed ceroids that are shrubby or sometimes tree-like. The areoles near the stem tips are cloaked in a dense mantle of white wool that protects both the fleshy, cup-shaped flowers and the ripening, red-pulped fruits. Flowers and fruit are nearly mature when they first peek through the protective wool, a sign that the fruit is almost ready to eat.

A related genus is *Cephalocereus*, as exemplified by the Mexican old man cactus, *C. senilis*—a very popular cactus, but a difficult one to grow. Its massive terminal cephalium, a woolly mass present only in mature plants, distinguishes it from other *Cephalocereus* species. Plantings in the Desert Garden are along the Golden Barrel Walk.

The green, fencepost-looking cacti behind the pincushion cacti are *Neobuxbaumia euphorbioides*, named for their resemblance to columnar euphorbias. The eight species of the genus *Neobuxbaumia* have flowers similar to the old man cactus and curious fruits that, when ripe, flare open like stars into five large segments to reveal the plant's juicy, seed-laden pulp.

One of the rarest cacti in the garden is an old, solitary neobuxbaumia on the path just north of the dragon tree. It may be the only specimen of *N. scoparia* in cultivation in the United States, making it the rarest of all cacti in the garden. Although its origin is unknown, it may be one of the plants Hertrich obtained in Mexico in 1912. Attempts to propagate it have been unsuccessful. It flowers yearly, in August, but does not set seed. It is native to Veracruz and Oaxaca, where it becomes a candelabrum-like monster nearly forty feet in height.

The Aztec column, *N. polylopha* (which means "many ribs"), is non-branching but has a thick telephone pole–like stem. Years ago, the oldest specimen in the garden had grown to thirty feet when a flicker created a nesting hole in the center of the plant, causing the top half to break off and crash to the ground. The Aztec column is one of the slowest-growing columnar cacti, with attractive pink blossoms.

The bluish, shrubby cacti at the upper end of the pincushion display are garambullo (*Myrtillocactus geometrizans*). The genus *Myrtillocactus* is common to much of Mexico and Baja California, and its species usually have a few thick, angled stems bearing short, stout spines. In Mexico, the plant's gooseberry-like fruits are considered a delicacy. The four species comprising the genus have several tiny whitish flowers per areole, a rare feature among cacti.

Throughout the garden are more than 500 specimens of golden barrel cactus (*Echinocactus grusonii*). Honoring Hermann Gruson, a nineteenth-century German cactus collector, the name gives little hint of the symmetrical beauty of the golden barrel. It is native to central Mexico, where it is endangered from over-collecting and development. The cactus's bright yellow spines are unsurpassed in their ornamental effect, but their functions are to reflect light, to form a protective, prickly shield to encase the plant body, and to direct moisture toward the roots. Buds develop beneath the woolly apex and, when mature, quickly emerge and open in dazzling yellow sunbursts. The ripe fruit is offered to birds for dispersal when it emerges from the protective wool.

The Huntington's golden barrel cacti are the largest to be seen anywhere. It is uncertain when the species was first introduced into the garden, but it is known that the largest specimens were grown from seed in the early 1920s and planted in 1929. Because the golden barrel is a major feature of the Desert Garden, new seedlings are planted at intervals to show various sizes.

April, May, and early June is flower season for most Northern Hemisphere cacti. It is also a good time to see—and photograph—the hedgehog cacti (*Echinocereus*), found in beds along the central path and lower Desert Garden. Hedgehogs were among the first cacti described in the early nineteenth century by botanists exploring the American West; many were discovered by those who were working on the railroad surveys. One of the most breathtaking flowering species is *E. pentalophus* (meaning "with five ribs"), a thin-stemmed, clustering cactus found below the garden's Baja California bed. In a good year, it is completely obscured by a mass of huge, brilliant pink flowers with whitish centers. Echinocerei are low-growing, inconspicuous plants, often hiding beneath shrubs, and their brilliant flowers attract pollinators from afar to their concealed and shaded habitat. *E. merkeri*, *E. salm-dyckianus*, and *E. scheeri* are displayed in the lower garden, affording unforgettable color with their bright pink and red-orange blossoms.

OPPOSITE ABOVE *Echinocereus pentalophus,*
Neobuxbaumia scoparia, E. scheeri var. *koerhesianus*
OPPOSITE BELOW *Myrtillocactus*
BELOW *Echinocactus grusonii* (golden barrel)

TERRESTRIAL BROMELIADS

THE TERRESTRIAL bromeliads of the pineapple family are exquisite in flower but seldom seen in landscaping. Unlike the tropical rainforest bromeliads that grow on other plants, these are semi-succulent, fibrous, agave-like plants that dwell in some of the most desolate regions of western South America. Bromeliad genera include *Puya, Dyckia, Hechtia, Abromeitiella,* and *Bromelia.*

Bromeliaceae is named after the seventeenth-century Swedish botanist Olaf Bromelius. *B. balansae* from Argentina and Paraguay, the famous "Heart of Fire," is planted above the upper garden entrance. Flowering is given advance notice by a spectacular color change in the inner leaf rosette from green to flaming red. A cluster of tightly compacted, tubular white flowers with scarlet edges emerges from the center of the plant, which dies after flowering. The heart of fire forms dense thickets and continues growing by means of thick, vigorous runners that have to be kept in check by gardeners. When the flowering ceases, the show continues with a third act, namely the production of a huge fruit mass of yellow, edible, hard-seeded fruits that taste like the pineapple, to which it is closely related.

TOP *Puya coerulea* var. *violacea*
ABOVE Puya flowerbuds
RIGHT *Bromelia balansae* 'Heart of Fire' before flowering, with flowers, and with fruit

Puya chilensis

T. Harper Goodspeed (see page 26) initiated the Huntington's bromeliad collection in the 1930s by donating seed that he had collected on his expeditions. One exception is the very large *Puya chilensis* at the bottom of the dragon tree bed, which was acquired in 1912. The puyas form the backbone of the bromeliad collection and put on a dramatic flourish of metallic turquoise and green color in the lower garden each April and May. *P. chilensis*, which forms massive clumps several meters across, and the smaller *P. alpestris* both produce dense, thorny rosettes of thin, narrow, fibrous leaves. *P. chilensis* and some others have thorns close to the leaf base that point inward and other thorns toward the outer end of the leaf that point outward. Thus, if an animal like a small rodent or lizard dares to penetrate the leaf's outer defense of thorns to feast on the succulent flower stalk, the inner thorns prevent it from escaping. Impaled on the leaf rosette, the animal dies and eventually decays, transforming into fertilizer for this passive green carnivore.

Puya flowers are one of the wonders of the plant world, for their branched flower stalks emerge from the

center of the plant to produce an abundant array of metallic blue, chartreuse, and violet flowers that have to be seen to be believed. Note the short floral branches in *P. alpestris*, and the fact that one-third of the branch has no flowers. This feature provides a perch for birds while they feast on the nectar. The comfortable accommodation ensures a long stay—the longer the birds remain, the more their heads will become thoroughly dusted with bright orange pollen.

P. mirabilis from Argentina and Bolivia is a grassy-leaved species that does not have the imposing presence of *P. chilensis*, yet yields some of the showiest blossoms in the genus. The flowers are very large, funnel-like, and pale chartreuse in color, opening at night and closing in the morning. Fortunately, April and May, its usual flowering months, tend to be overcast in Southern California, so this and many other so-called nocturnal flowering species remain open. *P. venusta*, an exquisite garden plant, has silvery-gray leaves and graceful, long-stalked clusters of deep purple flowers. It grows in the lower garden, where it forms a large, handsome, rounded clump.

The most remarkable and slowest-growing puya is the endangered *P. raimondii* from Peru. It grows at elevations of 13,000 feet in the Andes and develops for 100 years or more into a giant unbranched plant. Finally, it shoots up a gigantic fifteen-foot column of chartreuse flowers and then promptly dies. The garden's two plants are from seed collected in the wild, and their introduction to cultivation may be their only means of survival. *P. raimondii* has grown in the garden since 1962. In cultivation, it lives only twenty-five to thirty years, and its blooms are no match for those of the plants in their alpine habitat.

Dyckias, named after the early-nineteenth-century cactus enthusiast Prince Salm-Dyck of Germany, are semi-succulents found in the dry fields of Brazil, Paraguay, Argentina, and Bolivia. They are smaller and generally more succulent than puyas, and many, such as *Dyckia sulphurea* and *D. montevidensis* var. *rariflora*, form huge, stiff, leathery-leaved clumps or spreading ground covers. The flowers are borne on long, slender spikes in various shades of yellow.

One small bed in the garden contains a collection

TOP Flowers of *Puya chilensis, P. alpestris, P. venusta*
RIGHT *Dyckia maritima*

of hechtia, a terrestrial bromeliad from Mexico, particularly the Chihuahuan biome in north-central Mexico. One species, *Hechtia texensis*, is found in the Chihuahuan Desert of west Texas. Hechtia blossoms are inconspicuous but are borne on feathery blooms.

Some find the most curious hechtia to be *H. stenopetala*. It possesses an adaptive feature rarely observed in New World succulents—namely, a "window" effect that reduces light intensity on the upper leaf surface. The very sensitive photosynthetic tissues just beneath the underside of the leaf are protected from sun and heat damage by a thick, light-filtering layer extending for the full length of the upper side.

Abromeitiella is a delightful garden bromeliad, for its tiny dyckia-like leaf rosettes form tight, mossy cushions resembling rolling hills; it grows like a green glacier over rocks and other plants. *A. brevifolia* comes from the high Andes of northwest Argentina, and is seen in the garden opposite the pincushion rockery. Its metallic-green, tubular flowers barely peek beyond the leaf tips.

ABOVE RIGHT   *Abromeitiella brevifolia*
RIGHT   *Hechtia galeotti*

OCOTILLO

PLANTED AMONG the Mexican globular cacti and throughout the lower Desert Garden are several fouquierias, woody semi-succulent-to-succulent desert shrubs and small trees from Mexico and the Southwest United States. There are fifteen species and varieties, most of them growing in the garden. Certainly the best-known representative is the red-flowered coachwhip ocotillo, *Fouquieria splendens*, a tall shrub with long, wand-like stems arising from its base. But in the garden, the most striking fouquieria is the subtropical *F. diguetii*; many of these were grown from seed collected during botanical explorations in Mexico.

Fouquieria has an effective survival mechanism that allows them to suddenly develop and drop their leaves, depending on the presence of moisture. One leaf type is large, and when the leaf blade drops off, its stalk underneath becomes a thorn or spine. The other leaf type emerges directly from the stem and is a compacted branch consisting of a tiny leaf cluster called a fascicle. The flowers are tiny, five-parted, and appear in clusters. The common ocotillo and *F. diguetii*, or palo adán, have flame-red flowers.

Two species in the Mexican cactus rockeries are *F. purpusii* and *F. fasciculata*. Both are from central Mexico, and because of over-collecting are now endangered, particularly the former. The boojum-like *F. purpusii* specimens have been propagated from cuttings. *F. macdougallii*, located in the lower garden, is a short, thick-trunked shrub, and more squat than the common ocotillo of the Southwest; it is easier to grow and blooms more often. *F. formosa*, forming a grove along the Golden Barrel Walk, is a small tree with a beautiful trunk growing nearly twenty feet in height. Able to withstand light frost, it is excellent for landscaping, but its flowers are not as showy as the graceful *F. diguetii*.

Afternoon shade for the pincushion display is provided by a desert tree called the foothill palo verde (*Cercidium floridum*), a member of the pea family. The palo verde (meaning "green club") has photosynthetic tissue in its trunk and stems, permitting it to survive extreme drought. This palo verde and another showier sort, *Parkinsonia aculeata*, put on great displays of yellow flowers in early spring.

ABOVE *Fouquieria splendens*
OPPOSITE *Fouquieria diguetii*

SUCCULENTS OF BAJA CALIFORNIA

BAJA, OR LOWER, California—the 800-mile-long finger-like projection of California into Mexico—is one of the world's richest botanical regions for succulents. The Baja section of the Desert Garden contains nearly 100 species of succulents. One of its most impressive displays is the grove of boojum trees at the lower end of the bed. The Baja display also features the *datillo* (*Yucca valida*), a rockery planting of siempreviva (*Dudleya brittonii*), and the fearsome creeping devil (*Stenocereus eruca*), planted as an unfriendly ground cover.

The boojum, or cirio, consists of a single carrot-like stem projecting a myriad of small twiggy branches. In response to moisture, the stems produce tiny leaves like the other fouquierias. The boojum's odd branching habit leads some researchers to believe it a plant of great antiquity, perhaps developing during the Mesozoic Era over 100 million years ago. Three of the plants in the boojum grove date from the early Howard Gates expeditions to Baja in the early 1930s.

Y. valida, Baja's endemic tree yucca, forms miniature forests, as the plants arch downward and re-root, then sprout upward, creating an inchworm effect. *Y. valida* is known in Baja as *datillo*, meaning "little date," a reference to the plant's appearance. Its roots are used to make soap.

ABOVE LEFT *Yucca valida*
LEFT *Fouquieria columnaris* (boojum tree)
OPPOSITE The Baja section, with a comical grove
of *F. columnaris* and a cluster
of spiny *Opuntia invicta* at lower right

Dudleya brittonii, called siempreviva, belongs to the crassula family and grows along the northern Baja California coast. The white color of its leaves is from a thick coating of a light- and heat-reflecting, powdery, waxy deposit. Dudleyas are low-elevation relatives of echeveria, and their distribution extends into California and Arizona.

The creeping devil cactus (Stenocereus eruca) grows in the alluvial soils of Baja's Magdalena Plain. Its stems worm their way west over or around any object, growing at one end, dying at the other, and rooting as the growth inches forward. The creeping devil has delicate, white, fragrant flowers, but seldom blooms in cultivation. It is in danger of extinction, as much of its habitat is being bulldozed for agriculture. A shrubby S. eruca cousin is the pitaya agria, S. gummosus. Because of its chaotic growth, it is sometimes called the "galloping cactus." Its stems are used as fish poison by locals, but the fruit is edible.

One smaller cactus, the coast barrel (Ferocactus viridescens), is endangered in coastal Southern California but plentiful in Baja. Euphorbia xantii is a colorful landscape introduction forming a medium-to-large shrub with great masses of shocking pink-to-white blossoms several times a year.

ABOVE LEFT Dudleya brittoni
ABOVE RIGHT AND OPPOSITE
Stenocereus eruca
(creeping devil cactus)
RIGHT Ferocactus viridescens,
Euphorbia xantii
flowering in spring

LEFT *Opuntia macrocentra, O. basilaris*
BELOW *O. linguiformis* (cow's tongue cactus),
O. ellisiana, and *O. spinosior*

Throughout the Desert Garden are spiny cactus shrubs and small trees with flattened or circular stems resembling giant leaves. These species belong to the genus *Opuntia*, the best known of the cacti, the most adaptable, and the most widely distributed. There are at least 300 species, ranging from Canada to the southern tip of South America. Opuntias grow in all the states except those in New England. Sometimes they grow in such dense populations that they form impenetrable thickets. Many are naturalized in other parts of the world, including the Mediterranean, South Africa, and Australia.

Opuntias are one of the most easily recognizable cacti in the landscape. Their thick, flat stems, sometimes mistaken for leaves, are round or oval in outline, but very thin. Depending on the species, opuntias grow to form small clusters, like the beaver tail (*O. basilaris*), or branched shrubs (*O. ellisiana*), or even twenty-foot-tall trees such as *O. tomentosa*. The charming beaver tail is one of the more beautiful cacti in flower, with blossoms that resemble lovely pink roses.

TOP LEFT *Opuntia robusta*
ABOVE *O. erinacea* (grizzly bear cactus)

In contrast to the flat-stemmed opuntias are the cholla opuntias, called cylindropuntia, the tree-like cylindrical-stemmed cacti native to the Southwest and notorious for their barbed spines. Most are drab plants, like the buckhorn cholla (*Cylindropuntia versicolor*), which has surprisingly appealing flowers, or suspiciously attractive, like the grizzly bear cactus (*O. erinacea*), native to the Mojave desert. Nearly all opuntias have an uncanny ability to produce new roots on joints still on the plant, or after they detach and touch the ground. Many chollas native to the Southwest generate new growth when they drop their fruit. One curious feature of the opuntia is the presence of fleshy leaves in the new growth. The presence of such leaves indicates how primitive the genus is, and that it is more closely related to leafy pereskias than to barrel cacti.

TOP   Tunas on *Opuntia engelmannii*
ABOVE   *O. microdasys*

O. *ficus-indica* and O. *megacantha*, the mission cactus and the Indian fig cactus, are popular edible cacti in tropical America and the American Southwest. In both species, the freshly emerging growth and the fruits are edible. The new stems, called *nopales* in Spanish, are eaten raw in salads, pickled, or fried; the fruit, called *tunas*, can be eaten raw, prepared as a preserve, or even fermented into a wine. O. *megacantha*, native to Mexico, is regarded by some botanists as the original spiny form of the spineless O. *ficus-indica*, and both are found in the New World tropics. Although O. *megacantha* is regarded as having superior fruits, the mission fathers and early settlers widely distributed both sorts throughout the New World.

Another product associated with the mission cactus, and one that explains its presence in the Mediterranean region, is cochineal. Cochineal is a tiny, cottony, mealy bug that feeds on many kinds of opuntia. In the Desert Garden, the insects are attracted to O. *ficus-indica*, O. *megacantha*, and O. *ellisiana*, all three being attractive garden plants. The females exude a brilliant scarlet liquid that makes a red dye that was once coveted by pre-Colombian royalty in Mexico and Peru as well as Europe.

TOP   *Opuntia invicta*, O. *undulata*, and O. *microdasys* (crested bunny ears cactus)
ABOVE   Cochineal infestation on O. *ellisiana*
RIGHT   O. *littoralis* var. *austrocalifornica*

AGAVE AND AGAVE RELATIVES

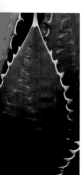

AGAVES ARE SEMI-SUCCULENT, fibrous plants with rosettes of tough leaves tipped with stout spines, a formidable armature of marginal thorns, and an irritating leaf juice. Sizes vary greatly, from the tiny *Agave parviflora*, a few inches across, to the giant *A. mapisaga* var. *lisa*, sixteen feet in breadth.

The agave family, Agavaceae, also includes such genera as yucca, dasylirion, beaucarnea, and nolina. The agave is of major economic importance globally for its tough fibers, used in rope and other woven products, and for its sap production. Its most crucial botanical features are its large tree-like flower stalk, seen in many agave species, or its spike- or feather-like cluster of flowers, seen in dasylirion or nolina; as well as its dry, capsular fruits with flat or winged seeds. Plants of most genera continue growing after flowering, but those in the genus *Agave* flower and die.

Agave and related genera are leaf succulents, in contrast to most cacti, which are stem succulents. They are also monocots, meaning they have fibrous, rather than woody, conducting tissue. During water stress, the rosette shrivels, drawing the leaves closer together, reducing water loss. As dead leaves break down around the base of the rosette, fibrous roots may grow from the base into the decayed leaves; thus, the larger agaves generate their own compost. When the agave is about to flower, the leaves at the swollen center of the plant quickly break apart, making way for an asparagus-like stalk. The emerging flower stalk completely transforms the leaf, producing a treelike cluster of flowers, gigantic in some species. The plant ends its life in glorious bloom. Some species produce no offsets, as is the case with most forms of the Queen Victoria agave (*A. victoriae-reginae*).

If an agave produces pups or offsets, a form of propagation frequently encountered in the genus, then only the flowering rosette dies. In dwarf species, the flower stalk may be only three or four feet high, but in the larger species, it is gigantic—as much as twenty or more feet tall. The flowers vary in color from dull white to deep orange or even red; they are filled with sweet nectar. The seeds are black and papery, and they are borne in dry, three-part capsules. Agaves grow throughout the Southwestern United States, Mexico, Central America, the West Indies, and Venezuela.

The common name for agave, "century plant," is a misnomer. It originated with the belief that potted specimens lived 100 years before flowering. Actually, when grown in the ground, the average agave's life span is only eight to twelve years, depending on the species. Some live twenty-five to forty-five years (such as *A. victoriae-reginae*), and container-bound specimens will put off flowering for what seems like a century.

TOP   Dried agave rosette, several months after flowering
ABOVE LEFT   *Agave horrida*

Agaves are more than decorative garden plants; they also serve as important life-support systems, providing food, moisture, and shelter for many animal species. Their sweet, nutritious nectar is crucial to the survival of many insects, birds, and small rodents, especially when there is little other available moisture. Were it not for the flowering activity of many species, some desert animals might not survive dry periods. In the Desert Garden, as many as a dozen hummingbirds zip around the large agave blooms, stopping just to guzzle the slightly fermented nectar, and, while under the influence, dive bomb any other of their kind trying to feed from the same plant. These hummingbirds are not alone: they are joined by multitudes of birds, bats, and bees.

TOP Variegated agaves
RIGHT *Agave shawii* var. *sebastiana* with its unusual flowering flat top

LEFT TO RIGHT *Agave* 'Boutin Blue,'
A. vilmoriniana (octopus agave)

Agaves in the Desert Garden reveal great variation in size and texture. For example, there are thornless agaves, such as the fox tail agave (*A. attenuata*), *A.* 'Boutin Blue', octopus agave (*A. vilmoriniana*), and *A. bracteosa*. *A.* 'Boutin Blue' (after former Huntington botanist, Fred Boutin, its discoverer) has blue leaves and a full, upright cluster of flowers that makes it much showier than *A. attenuata*.

A. bracteosa has the most distinctive bloom, with a six-foot pillar of thousands of soft creamy-white blossoms; it is best seen in May and June. The *A. vilmoriniana* bloom is equally dramatic, with a bright yellow flower on a slender fifteen-foot stalk. After the flowers wither and drop away, the stalk transforms itself to green with the appearance of hundreds of tiny plantlets. Agaves survive in one of two ways: if environmental conditions are such that the seeds cannot germinate, there are plantlets that are complete with roots. As the flower stalk dies, the plantlets detach, fall to the ground, and take root.

Occasionally a visitor asks about some curious tree in the Desert Garden. Actually, they are not trees at all, but rather the huge branched flower stalks of the larger agaves. These have ten- to twelve-foot open rosettes of deep to pale green floppy or erect leaves, and include *A. ferox*, *A. salmiana*, *A. inaequidens*, *A. mapisaga* var. *lisa*, and *A. ragusae*. Not all agaves are green giants: *A. franzosinii*, for instance, has broad, chalky gray leaves. The best specimens in the garden are the sentinels framing the Oxford Road entrance to the Huntington; the others are seen in the lower Desert Garden.

A. americana is a longtime favorite that is naturalized in some parts of Southern California and may have been introduced in the eighteenth century. In Mexico, it is also used in pulque production. It is six to seven feet tall and has broad, gray leaves. The equally popular variegated form, *A. americana* 'Marginata,' has bright yellow leaf margins. Occasionally the margin colors reverse, with the green

LEFT TO RIGHT
A. bracteosa, mature specimen of
A. mapisaga var. *lisa*

on the outside and yellow as the midstripe (as in *A. americana* var. *medio-picta*).

Medium agaves—that is, those less than four feet in diameter—are represented in the garden by the long-lived *A. parryi* var. *huachucensis*, native to Arizona, New Mexico, and Chihuahua, Mexico. It forms a dense, artichoke-like rosette of gray, short, stiff leaves tipped with a stout, dark spine. When its bright orange flowers appear, it is transformed into one of the most beautiful agaves in the garden. This decorative effect is exceeded by another Huntington introduction, the sculpture-like, bluish-leaved *A. parryi* var. *truncata*.

Small agaves are those less than two feet in diameter. One gorgeous example is *A. ocahui*, which forms a many-leaved, tight rosette. It is closely related to the octopus agave, *A. vilmoriniana*. Another is the clump-forming *A. filifera*, named for its long, peeling marginal leaf fibers. The presence of a delightfully attractive white decorative banding on the leaf underside is a curious phenomenon— it is splendidly developed in the exotic Queen Victoria agave, *A. victoriae-reginae*. Its flower stalk is a ten-foot spike of purplish flowers with extra-long stamens that give it a fuzzy appearance.

CLOCKWISE FROM TOP LEFT
Agave americana 'Variegated,' *A. victoriae-reginae*,
A. parryi var. *truncata*, and *A. ocahui*

TOP   Pulque agave
LEFT   *Agave fourcroydes*

Fiber, pulque, and tequila agaves are among the several hundred collections in the Desert Garden. Flowering agaves are best seen in spring and summer, but a few species bloom in autumn and winter.

Agave leaf fiber was widely used in pre-Colombian times and still is today. Before the arrival of the Europeans, the Mayans and Aztecs used the fiber for skirts, sandals, nets, baskets, and a variety of other woven objects. The well-known sisal and henequen rope are made from agave fiber—particularly from *A. sisalana* and *A. fourcroydes*, respectively. In Mexico and Central America the leaves are used for roofing and fencing. The center section of the plant with all its leaves removed, called the *cabeza*, is roasted to convert its starch to a thick, molasses-like energy food.

The agave has a long, colorful history as the source of a mildly alcoholic beverage called pulque, which is the fermented leaf juice. There is evidence that pulque has been used in Mexico for thousands of years. Today pulque is imbibed only when fresh and is served in local pulquerias.

The largest agaves—*A. atrovirens*, *A. mapisaga* var. *lisa*, and similar species—are important pulque producers. Another agave beverage is mescal, developed by early Spanish colonists when their supply of European liquor dried up. Mescal contains more alcohol than pulque. It is not distilled from pulque agaves, as is commonly thought, but rather from different species, such as *A. mescal*. Production requires cutting away all the leaves until only the base remains. The *piña*, or heart, is chopped, roasted, and distilled to get the clear mescal.

Whoever drinks a shot of tequila or sips a margarita has firsthand knowledge of the potent double-distilled juices of *A. tequilana*. There is a specimen on the central path in the lower garden.

Humans also use the agave as a food source. For thousands of years, Amerindians have incorporated agave products into their diets and material economy, consuming the emerging flower stalk and heart of the plant. Agaves may also have pharmacological properties, like the decorative *A. vilmoriniana*, which produces useful compounds for cortisone synthesis.

ABOVE Leaves of *Agave fourcroydes* are an important source of commercial fiber

Furcraea is a conspicuous agave relative and the most difficult one to distinguish from the genus *Agave*. It is less succulent and its distribution is more tropical—namely, the Caribbean and tropical America. Like the agave, it flowers and then dies. Some species, such as *F. selloa-marginata*, found across from the garden's pincushion rockery, send up huge fountains of hundreds of whitish bell-shaped flowers. After flowering, this twenty-foot tree-like stalk is so weighted down with hundreds of plantlets that it often collapses under the weight of its progeny—by now a veritable forest in a flower stalk. *F. roezlii* and *F. macdougallii* may grow to twenty feet before flowering, when they generate magnificent Christmas tree–like flower stalks at least twenty-five feet in height. These are possibly the tallest flower stalks in the agave family.

Hesperaloe means Western aloe, but it is actually in the agave family. In contrast to agave, hesperaloe does not die with a final flowering; instead, it branches from its base and continues growing. *H. parviflora* is much used in Southwest landscaping and is well known for its showy pink flowers. Its leaves are smooth with long marginal threads. In the garden, the hesperaloes, including the long-leaved furcraea-like *H. funifera*, appear along the Golden Barrel Walk.

Hertrich's epochal 1912 collecting trip to Mexico yielded carloads of cacti and other succulents, including the gigantic *Yucca filifera* in the lower end of the garden. Some of these are tree-like and well over thirty feet in height. Native to north-central Mexico, they are much larger than the California native Joshua tree (*Y. brevifolia*). Yuccas are pollinated by the pronuba moth, a small nondescript insect that collects pollen from the flower as it lays its eggs on the stigma; the hatchlings develop into grubs and eat their way into the flower's ovary beneath the stigma to feed on the ovules. Yuccas are well known to botany students, for the pollination of their attractive (and edible) bell-shaped flowers is a textbook example of a symbiotic—that is, mutually beneficial—relationship between plant and animal.

ABOVE *Furcraea selloa-marginata, F. roezlii*
LEFT *F. macdougalli*

On the west side of the garden near Palm Garden Drive and the huge dragon tree are specimens of the unusual bear grass tree (*Nolina longifolia*) and the bottle tree (*Beaucarnea stricta*), both from Mexico and early residents of the garden. These are large, fibrous, semi-succulent trees with dense, grassy rosettes of thin, saw-toothed leaves. Their trunks are thick and swollen (fantastically so in beaucarnea) and generally have corky or deeply furrowed bark.

The bear grass tree is squat and parasol shaped, with leaves up to six feet long cascading from its crown. *N. matapensis* is a more recent discovery. Slender and more graceful than *N. longifolia*, it was long lost to botanists until a Huntington expedition rediscovered it in a secluded canyon in northern Sonora, Mexico.

B. recurvata, best known in the trade as the ponytail palm (even though it is not a palm), is used in Southern California landscaping as an eye-catching accent. A grove near the Palm Garden shows how their fantastic shapes transform the landscape into a Dr. Seuss–like fairytale garden. Their trunks are enormous reservoirs of stored moisture, and they taper to thin, graceful branches topped by clusters of hanging leaves. This grove contains some of the oldest plants in the garden. *B. recurvata* likes water and is easily grown from seed.

Among the cacti in the lower garden's Sonoran display is the strange grassy nolina relative, *Calibanus hookeri*, named after the ugly and distorted Caliban in Shakespeare's *The Tempest*. Like the dioscorea, described on page 51, it has an enormous succulent base. It is covered with short, stiff, grass-like leaves, but its tiny seeds are not winged as they are in nolina.

TOP *Nolina matapensis*
ABOVE *Yucca filifera* flower
OVERLEAF LEFT *Beaucarnea recurvata*
with *Agave murpheyi* 'Variegated' in
foreground, RIGHT *Y. filifera*,
planted in 1912

The World *of the* Desert Garden

THE HUNTINGTON'S DESERT GARDEN departs from many conventional traditions of design, upkeep, and purpose. This section discusses some of the problems of care, and how to keep alive and healthy so many different kinds of succulents in close quarters. Docents like to talk to visitors about the garden's history as well as how desert plants survive lack of water, intense heat, and even cold, as well as water and food seeking predators. This is not a conventional public garden; it serves many purposes and needs with its Ark project, the most recent example (see page 112).

LEFT A colorful display of
aloes and ice plants
TOP *Mammillaria magnimamma*
ABOVE Brilliant yellow aeonium flowers

CARE OF THE DESERT GARDEN

Tending nearly twelve acres of cactus isn't everyone's dream: a false step while gardening in the mammillaria bed or loss of balance while weeding the creeping devil cacti could be a painful nightmare. Working among the cacti in steep rockeries seems life threatening, and there have been scary moments when a curator or gardener gets trapped by heavily armed branches and is unable to move forward or backward. Gardeners and volunteers must be as sure footed as mountain goats, as a slip can result in a painful, humiliating fall on a treacherous cactus.

And yet, the cultivation of such a diverse, historic landscape requires that much of the work be done by hand, including weeding, watering, pruning, planting, transplanting, propagating, and landscaping. It is the curator's responsibility to ensure that the garden is kept to the highest standard of excellence possible, which includes labeling, planting, transplanting, and rescuing poorly performing plants. Sometimes tools have to be modified, or even invented, in order to cultivate plants that would cause severe injury if they were handled with traditional garden tools.

One of the secrets of weeding is to do so after heavy rains or deep waterings. Weeding implements include dandelion diggers, asparagus cutters, medical tweezers, screwdrivers, and a variety of homemade sharpened devices, all with the intent to remove weeds around plants that are well armed against intrusion into their space. In a subtropical climate, the weed season is all year. A variety of species invade the garden in waves, most notably with the onset of fall or winter rains. Early-, mid-, and late-season annual grasses, mustard, plus a variety of composite weeds such as dandelion continue into summer. Heat and humidity brings forth spurge and purslane. In the fall, bulbs of

RIGHT
Echium wildpretii
plant, flower
stalk, and flowers

Puya flowers

Moraea polystachya, the African iris, awaken from dormancy, sending up showy blue flowers unpredictably throughout the garden. They are one of the "accidents" that contribute to the garden's beauty.

New pre-emergent weed killers are being cautiously tested in some parts of the garden. Years ago it was utilized routinely, but it prevented germination of the native yucca, *Y. whipplei*, which for years was naturalized in the lower Desert Garden. Now it no longer comes up in the garden.

The practice of deadheading helps to define plant shapes in the garden as well as the intensity of plant color and texture. Cutting away dry flower stalks gives a clear picture of the plant and its visual impact. In many succulents, the accumulation of dried flower stalks, flower and fruit parts, and dried leaves provides shade and protection, but in a landscape garden, this detracts from the display. Today's formalism survives more in the form of grooming practices rather than from geometric rock arrangement. A few dried flower stalks, particularly agave and yucca, are always left in the garden, both for aesthetic reasons and to provide perches for birds.

Some plants are encouraged to set seed in the hope that they will reproduce. Some of the large cerei in the garden are volunteers dating from the 1920s. Palo verde and desert willow appear in various spots as seedling volunteers, as well as the biennial tower of jewels (*Echium wildpretii*) from the Canary Islands. The California native St. Catherine's lace (*Eriogonum giganteum*) reproduces from seed and has done so for over fifty years.

Most of the succulents that are destined for the Desert Garden are grown and propagated in the Desert Collections Nursery. They are then planted in the garden during warm periods, usually in spring and fall. The testing, observing, and evaluating of newly introduced species and cultivars—a practice begun by Hertrich—continues to this day. For years Hertrich kept meticulous records, including photographs, of the flowering and fruiting activities of some night-blooming cereus, opuntia, hybrid aloes, and other plants that showed horticultural promise for Southern California gardens. His observations of citrus and avocado plantings at the Huntington contributed to the development of both industries in Southern California. In order for succulents to perform as suitable plants for the landscape, they must grow well in hot- and cold-weather conditions. Some succulents, such as adenium, will not tolerate temperatures much below 50 degrees, while some hedgehog cacti would flower better if they have a good winter chill—fortunately for the other plants, a rare event.

Planting, transplanting, and propagation in the garden begins in March or April. Occasionally a new or interesting species is tested, such as the brilliant red-orange flowering *Aloe porphyrostachys* from Arabia, which performs quite well. In late April and early May, the puyas put on one of the most unusual floral displays to be seen anywhere. Their spectacular floral spires and branched stalks of metallic turquoise, viridian, indigo, purple, magenta, and pink blossoms contain sweet nectar and copious pollen that attract numerous kinds of birds.

In spring, small cacti are planted in the rockeries along the central path. A balanced, slow-release fertilizer is included in the backfill. Burying the fertilizer means the nutrient goes to the cactus, not to the weeds, which would produce luxuriant growth if a liquid fertilizer were applied. Plants are fertilized infrequently, in order to encourage heat- and cold-tolerant growth rather than speedy, lush growth. Efforts to introduce appropriate shade plants for the cacti have met with limited success, as it seems many South American cacti are sensitive to California's hot afternoon sun. Plants are placed adjacent to rocks to make it appear as if the plants grew naturally from those spots. Observing how cacti grow in the wild is one way to become educated about rockery planting. Open, well-drained soil anchored to and protected by stone enables survival in the wild and makes a botanical display that contributes to the understanding of adaptation to aridity.

Agaves grow best if they are planted in the spring. If small plants are put in the ground in the fall, they can perish from heavy winter rains. Before planting, the Huntington's records are checked to see how big the agave grows and whether it spreads by offsets or grows as a single rosette. A single rosette means it will eventually flower and die. An offsetting agave such as *A. lechuguilla* covers large areas, just as it covers parts of the Chihuahuan desert. Generally, agaves grow well in sandy loam without any soil amendment or fertilizer. They do thrive with full sun and ample water. If agaves are overfertilized and overwatered, their size can greatly exceed that seen in the wild. Howard Scott Gentry often complained that the agaves in the Huntington were so lush that they defied accurate description.

ABOVE   Agave flower stalk
RIGHT   *Agave sisalana* 'Variegated'

ARIDITY AND SURVIVAL

When visitors to the Huntington's Desert Garden find themselves surrounded by this lush tropical or subtropical paradise planted in succulents, they might be tempted to believe they are looking at plants that thrive in the deserts of the Southwest. On the contrary, many of the plants grown in the Desert Garden are not found in harsh deserts. Arid drylands such as the Los Angeles basin are not associated with the desert, even though they have periods of little or no rainfall. Cacti, other succulents, and yuccas grow naturally there, but it is not a desert in a strict sense. Therefore, why not call the garden an exotic succulent garden? One could say that the Desert Garden more closely represents a succulent Garden of Eden than it does the Mojave or Sonoran deserts. Its biome, or ecological community, is variously called oak scrub, oak woodland, oak grassland, chaparral, or sage scrub. As a landscaped botanical garden, it does not pretend to reproduce the nearby desert biome.

True deserts receive less than ten inches of rain per year as well as extended periods of severe drought and extreme temperatures. For example, the Mojave Desert, the desert nearest to the Huntington, rarely experiences summer rainfall and is known for its low humidity and cold winters. The Mojave receives only two to ten inches of rain in the winter, rarely any in the summer, and its temperatures range from near zero to 130 degrees Fahrenheit. These conditions would be too harsh for most of the succulents in the Desert Garden. If such a garden were to be planted in Barstow, 115 miles northeast of Los Angeles, at least ninety-five percent of it would not survive.

As one travels east from the Mediterranean coastal area of Southern California, the climate transitions dramatically, from mild, salubrious weather to an intense dry heat with windy conditions, to below-freezing temperatures that can include snow. In this harsh desert, one finds the compass barrel cacti, teddy bear cholla, Engelmann hedgehog, Joshua tree, and ocotillo. None of these species thrives at the Huntington—or in coastal Southern California, for that matter.

Therefore, in describing succulent habitat, one should speak not so much of desert, but rather of irregular, unpredictable, spotty, or seasonal availability of life-sustaining water. Xerophytes are plants that are capable of conserving life-giving moisture, and most of these are succulents.

So where do the Desert Garden's 4,000 species of succulents originate? Many of the North American succulents in the Desert Garden are found in pine oak woodlands or dry thorn forests, such as the highlands and lowlands of Mexico, which experience monsoon conditions and occasional hurricanes. Closer to the equator, where climatic conditions become less extreme, rainfall may be spotty throughout the year. Below the equator lie fog deserts (where plants receive most of their moisture from fog), coastal sage, chaparral, grassland, and even tropical jungle. Some of the garden's South American cacti are best regarded as sub-alpine and even alpine, since they grow at elevations of over 12,000 feet in the Andes.

ABOVE The Desert Garden in 1974

What is Succulence? Succulence is an adaptive strategy for survival. Wherever unpredictable or seasonal rainfall occurs, and drainage and soil conditions are appropriate, thick-stemmed, juicy-leaved plants have adapted to survive drought, as have other types of plants. Succulence is not a plant family, but rather a mode of enduring adverse conditions or the absence of moisture. A plant must conserve and store its own water supply in order to survive in the Southwest deserts, the Pacific Coast, the Rocky Mountains, the Peruvian Andes, the highlands and lowlands of Mexico, and the American, South American, and African grasslands. Oddly, Southern California, because of its milder temperatures, provides a more suitable environment for cultivating a wider variety of succulent species than does the sizzling Mojave Desert on the other side of the San Gabriel Mountains. The major aspect that makes an environment favorable to succulence is simply the absence of continuous or predictable rainfall.

Most stem succulents have devices—such as an armature of spines—that protect the plant from predators and other stresses, including the hot sun. Spines and hairs shade the plant from intense light and insulate it from both heat and cold. Some cacti, such as the so-called jumping cholla, use their barbed spines and detachable stems as a means of dispersal that becomes readily attached to any animal that happens to brush up against the plant. African succulents such as adenium and euphorbia have poisonous sap that can cause severe injury if ingested.

How Plants Adapt to Aridity. Succulents adapt to dry conditions through a variety of strategies. Some take in moisture and store it in their stems, leaves, or roots, or all three. Others have a reduced amount of surface area or a smaller number of stomata, or pores, that release water through evaporation and plant transpiration. Strategies include:

- Thick succulent leaves are arranged in tight rosettes that expose only a portion of each leaf to sunlight (such as *Aeonium tabulaeforme*).
- The number and size of leaves is reduced, or leaves are absent altogether (such as *Euphorbia obesa*).
- Ephemeral leaves wither in the absence of moisture (such as *Opuntia*).
- A fan-like leaf arrangement compresses under stress to reduce the amount of surface area so that less water is released (such as *Aloe plicatilis*).
- A spherical ribbed plant body expands and contracts, adding to or reducing the amount of surface area (such as a golden barrel cactus). In terms of geometric figures, the sphere is the one with the least amount of surface area for a given volume.
- Photosynthesis occurs in thick, ribbed succulent columns rather than in leaves (such as *Pachycereus marginatus*).
- Roots contract to pull the plant partially or entirely into the ground, thereby reducing the exposed surface area (such as *Ariocarpus*).
- Large roots, tubers or swollen trunks store moisture (such as *Ficus petiolaris*).

- Dense coverings of wool, hairs, and bristles protect the plant from sunlight (such as *Oreocereus*).
- A waxy cuticle and a thickened epidermis prevent water loss (such as *Senecio*).
- An armature of spines or thorns shades the surface and repels predators (such as *Stenocereus eruca*).
- Toxic stem sap repels grazers (such as *Euphorbia*).
- Moisture translocates from the atmosphere directly through the stem or leaf surface (such as *Welwitschia*).
- The plant switches from diurnal photosynthesis to nocturnal photosynthesis (such as *Crassula*).

Succulents are generally shallow-rooted to allow for quick moisture absorption. Their native soils tend to be well drained—that is, the soil is open or sandy, and water is quickly drained away from the roots. Others grow in rock-hard, undrained clay, yet survive because rain is extremely rare.

Many globular succulents have fluted or columnar stems that permit the plant to expand or contract based on the availability of moisture. The genus *Cereus* and related genera grouped as ceroids provide fine examples. Some highly specialized species, such as the rock-like cactus called *Ariocarpus*, have thick taproots that contract to pull the plant beneath the soil surface, protecting it from the ravages of drought. In many cases, the color and shape of the plant offers camouflage so effective that some species can be found only when in flower. Leaf succulents expand or contract (or shrivel) their leaves depending on water availability, often overlapping or curling them over the center of the rosette to shade and protect the topmost part of the shoot from heat and predator damage.

Another survival strategy clearly seen in large golden barrels and other cacti is the presence of wool. This insulating wool protects tender new growth, flower buds, and immature fruits. The wool not only protects the plant from the desiccating effects of the hot sun, but also conceals tender parts from hungry predators.

OPPOSITE Agave, *Coryphantha pulleineana*
ABOVE *Dactylopsis digitata*, *Cheiridopsis peculiaris*, and *Pachycereus gaumeri*
LEFT Boojum trees, golden barrel cacti

PROTECTING PLANT DIVERSITY

 WHILE PROTECTIVE MEASURES must be taken to conserve plants in their habitats, a botanical garden such as the Huntington's Desert Garden can play a valuable role in propagating and distributing documented genetic material to other gardens, the public, and to restoration projects. As an older garden, it contains a rich storehouse of species introduced to the Huntington forty to one hundred years ago. Some of these species, like *Cereus xanthocarpus*, are little known, even unknown, to cultivation.

The Desert Garden and its inventory, much of it not on public view, comprise a treasure house of rare species and genetic components. Many of the plants in the collection are not widely cultivated elsewhere, and some have never been properly identified. The garden is based on not only ornamental, commercially grown materials, but also on specific plants and seeds that were collected and documented from the wild. Some of the materials were gathered more a century ago, from habitats that may no longer exist. One of the Desert Garden's goals is to conserve these botanical treasures in perpetuity.

The Huntington has an ex situ conservation program called the Botanical Ark, which identifies plants, including those in the Desert Garden and collection, that have scientific, medicinal, food, economic, or historic value. The Ark is a program that identifies and propagates rare, endangered, and significant plants in the garden and collection. This is supported through existing programs such as the public Desert Conservatory plus a greenhouse collection and a plant introduction program.

Though we have mentioned only a handful of the dozens of plant families represented in the Desert Garden, it is hoped that this guide will give the visitor an introduction to some of the Huntington's botanical treasures. The garden, visually at its best in the cool of late afternoon, or, during the summer months, in the morning, presents a unique vision of Eden, one that testifies to a century of sheer survival as well as the loving and conscientious care of its gardeners.

ABOVE *Aloe suprafoliata* flower
OPPOSITE *Cereus xanthocarpus*, acquired in 1912, is the oldest cactus in the Desert Garden. Near the end of its lifespan, this specimen may be the only known example of this species in cultivation.

ACKNOWLEDGMENTS

FIRST AND FOREMOST I wish to express my appreciation and thanks for the dedication and hard work of the Desert Garden's five gardeners: Martin Coronado, Faustino Benites, Juan "Pancho" Sanchez, Adolfo Alvarez, and Michael Romero. Martin has taken care of the Desert Garden for forty years and is a living lesson in dedication. Myron Kimnach, curator emeritus, mentored and encouraged me through my many years at the Huntington. My sincere thanks go to Marge and Sherm Telleen for their generous support of the garden, and I want especially to thank Joan and David T. Traitel for their generous support for the renovation of the Desert Garden's Heritage Walk. I must give thanks to Jim Folsom, director of the Huntington Botanical Gardens, for his support and enthusiasm for the Desert Garden, and to John Trager, curator of the Desert Collections. Of course, I have to thank John Sullivan, Huntington photographer, who took some spectacular photos with his Hasselblad camera. Additionally I must thank Peggy Bernal, director of Huntington Library Press, and production editor Jean Patterson.

There are many who encouraged me and gave wise counsel to bring to fruition the first Desert Garden book published by the Huntington. Most notably, I give special thanks and gratitude to Kathryn Philipps, who generously shared her archival research on the Desert Garden's beginnings. Katheryn Venturelli is owed a great debt of gratitude for her assistance is preparing the manuscript for submission. I want to thank Jennifer Watts, curator of photographs; Alan Jutzi, chief curator of rare books; and Dan Lewis, curator of the history of science and technology, for encouraging me to study the garden's history. I am also grateful for the encouragement and support of the following: Patrick Anderson, Christle Balvin, Tim Brick, Pat and Jack Crowther, Joanne Gram, Kelly Kimball and the Kimball clan, Marian and Phil Kovinick, Tabitha Morris, Barbara Quinn, Ann Scheid, Phil Skoniecski, Kylee Smith, Anthony Weller, Michelle Zack, and Karen Zimmerman.

Finally, I must acknowledge an enormous debt of gratitude to William Hertrich: his inspiration and guiding spirit taught me to plant my prayers rather than say them.

Gary Lyons
Curator of the Desert Garden

OPPOSITE Flowering lampranthus seedlings on a sunny day; behind is the menacing, sharp-leaved heart of flame, *Bromelia balansae*.

BIBLIOGRAPHY

Albers, Focke, and Ulrich Meve, eds. *Illustrated Handbook of Succulent Plants: Asclepiadaceae*. Berlin, Heidelberg, and New York: Springer-Verlag, 2002.

Anderson, Edward F. *The Cactus Family*. Portland, Ore.: Timber Press, 2001.

Anderson, Edward F., Salvador Arias Montes, and Nigel P. Taylor. *Threatened Cacti of Mexico*. London: Royal Botanic Gardens, 1994.

Anderson, Miles, and Terry Hewitt. *The World Encyclopedia of Cacti & Succulents*. London: Hermes House, 1999.

Benson, Lyman David. *The Cacti of the United States and Canada*. Stanford, Calif.: Stanford University Press, 1982.

Britton, Nathaniel Lord, and Joseph Nelson Rose. *The Cactaceae: Descriptions and Illustrations of Plants in the Cactus Family*. 4 vols. Washington, D.C.: The Carnegie Institution of Washington, 1919–23.

Cave, Yvonne. *Succulents for the Contemporary Garden*. Portland, Ore.: Timber Press, 2003.

Eggli, Urs, ed. *Illustrated Handbook of Succulent Plants: Crassulaceae*. Berlin, Heidelberg, and New York: Springer-Verlag, 2003.

——. *Illustrated Handbook of Succulent Plants: Dicotyledons*. Berlin, Heidelberg, and New York: Springer-Verlag, 2002.

Gentry, Howard Scott. *Agaves of Continental North America*. Tucson, Ariz.: University of Arizona Press, 1982.

Grantham, Keith, and Paul Klaassen. *The Plantfinder's Guide to Cacti & Other Succulents*. Portland, Ore.: Timber Press, 1999.

Hartmann, Heidrun E. K., ed. *Illustrated Handbook of Succulent Plants: Aizoaceae*. 2 vols. Berlin, Heidelberg, and New York: Spring-Verlag, 2002.

Herre, Hans. *The Genera of the Mesembryanthemaceae*. Rotterdam, Holland: A. A. Balkema, 1979.

Hertrich, William. *The Huntington Botanical Gardens 1905–1949*. San Marino, Calif.: Henry E. Huntington Library and Art Gallery, 1949.

——. *A Guide to the Desert Plant Collection in the Huntington Botanical Gardens*. San Marino, Calif.: Henry E. Huntington Library and Art Gallery, 1937.

Houk, Rose. *Wild Cactus*. Photographs by George H. H. Huey. New York: Artisan, 1996.

Hunt, David, comp. and ed. *The New Cactus Lexicon*. 2 vols. Milborne Port, U.K.: dh books, 2006.

Irish, Mary and Gary Irish. *Agaves, Yuccas, and Related Plants: A Gardener's Guide*. Portland, Ore.: Timber Press, 2000.

Jeppe, Barbara. *South African Aloes*. Cape Town, South Africa, and London: Purnell, 1969.

OPPOSITE *Euphorbia milii* var. *hislopii*

Kapitany, Attila, and Rudolf Schulz. *Succulents for the Garden.* Revised ed. Teesdale, Australia: Schulz Publishing, 2006.

———. *Succulents: Propagation.* Succulents for the Garden Series. Teesdale, Australia: Schulz Publishing, 2004.

———. *Succulents: Care and Health.* Succulents for the Garden Series. Teesdale, Australia: Schulz Publishing, 2003.

———. *Succulent Success in the Garden.* Succulents for the Garden Series. Teesdale, Australia: Schulz Publishing, 2002.

———. *More Succulents for the Garden.* Succulents for the Garden Series. Teesdale, Australia: Schulz Publishing, 2001.

Lowell, Susan. *Cactus Flowers.* Look West Series. Tucson, Ariz.: Rio Nuevo Publishers, 2005.

Lyons, Gary. *Desert Gardens.* Photographs by Melba Levick. New York: Rizzoli, 2000.

———. *The Huntington Desert Garden.* Reseda, Calif.: Abbey Garden Press, 1969.

Mace, Tony, and Suzanne Mace. *Cactus Basics: A Comprehensive Guide to Cultivation and Care.* London: Hamlyn, 2006.

Manke, Elisabeth. *Cactus: The Most Beautiful Varieties and How to Keep Them Healthy.* Hauppauge, N.Y.: Barron's Educational Series, 2000.

McKelvey, Susan Delano. *Yuccas of the Southwestern United States.* 2 vols. Jamaica Plain, Mass.: Arnold Arboretum of Harvard University, 1937–38.

Morhardt, Sia, and Emil Morhardt. *California Desert Flowers: An Introduction to Families, Genera, and Species.* Berkeley and Los Angeles: University of California Press, 2004.

Padilla, Victoria. *Southern California Gardens: An Illustrated History.* Berkeley and Los Angeles: University of California Press, 1961.

Preston-Mafham, Rod, and Ken Preston-Mafham. *Cacti: The Illustrated Dictionary.* Reprint. Portland, Ore.: Timber Press, 1997.

Quinn, Meg. *Cacti of the Desert Southwest.* Tucson, Ariz.: Rio Nuevo Publishers, 2001.

Rauh, Werner. *Succulent and Xerophytic Plants of Madagascar.* 2 vols. Mill Valley, Calif.: Strawberry Press, 1995–98.

Reynolds, Gilbert Westacott. *The Aloes of South Africa.* Reprint. Cape Town, South Africa: A. A. Balkema, 1969.

———. *The Aloes of Tropical Africa and Madagascar.* Mbabane, Swaziland: Trustees of the Aloes Book Fund, 1966.

Rogers, Ray, ed. *Crazy about Cacti and Succulents.* Brooklyn Botanic Garden All-Region Guide. Brooklyn, N.Y.: Brooklyn Botanic Garden, 2006.

Rowley, Gordon Douglas. *Crassula: A Grower's Guide*. Milan, Italy: Cactus and Company libri, 2003.

——. *A History of Succulent Plants*. Mill Valley, Calif.: Strawberry Press, 1997.

——. *The Illustrated Encyclopedia of Succulents*. New York: Crown Publishers, 1978.

Sajeva, Maurizio, and Mariangela Costanzo. *Succulents: The Illustrated Dictionary*. Portland, Ore.: Timber Press, 1997.

Smith, Gideon F. *Succulents II: The New Illustrated Dictionary*. Succulents Series. Portland, Ore.: Timber Press, 2000.

Smith, Gideon F., et al. *Mesembs of the World*. Pretoria, South Africa: Briza Publications, 1998.

Spurgeon, Selena A. *Henry Edwards Huntington: His Life and His Collections, A Docent Guide*. Reprint. San Marino, Calif.: Huntington Library, 2002.

Stephenson, Ray. *Sedum: Cultivated Stonecrops*. Portland, Ore.: Timber Press, 1994.

Thorpe, James. *Henry Edwards Huntington: A Biography*. Berkeley, Los Angeles, and London: University of California Press, 1994.

Thorpe, James, Robert R. Wark, and Ray Allen Billington. *The Founding of the Henry E. Huntington Library and Art Gallery*. San Marino, Calif.: Huntington Library, 1969.

Truman, Benjamin C. *Semi-Tropical California*. San Francisco: A. L. Bancroft and Co., 1874.

Van Wyck, Ben-Erik, and Gideon Smith. *Guide to the Aloes of South Africa*. 2nd ed. Pretoria, South Africa: Briza Publications, 2003.

White, Alain, R. Allen Dyer, and Boyd L. Sloane. *The Succulent Euphorbieae (Southern Africa)*. 2 vols. Pasadena, Calif.: Abbey Garden Press, 1941.

OVERLEAF   Golden barrel cacti

INDEX

DESIGNERS ARE often the invisible partner in the production of books. But in the case of this book, the Huntington would like to call special attention to the designer, Lilli Colton, without whose vision the book simply would not have been possible. She miraculously and thoughtfully transformed a complicated mélange of text and pictures into what we hope you will agree is an attractive and informative presentation.

DESERT PLANTS: A CURATOR'S INTRODUCTION
TO THE HUNTINGTON DESERT GARDEN

was produced on the centennial of one of the world's preeminent desert plant collections and a popular and botanically important garden at the Huntington. The book was designed by Lilli Colton and typeset in Sabon, with headings in Formata and display type in Centaur. A first edition of 3000 softcover and 1000 casebound books was printed in Pasadena, California by Typecraft Wood & Jones.

A mockingbird
perches on a branch of
Cereus pseudocaesius,
one of the oldest
columnar cacti in the
Desert Garden.